KU-542-525

GOOD NEWS
TOLD BY MATTHEW

Today's English Version

THE BRITISH AND
FOREIGN BIBLE SOCIETY

THE NATIONAL BIBLE
SOCIETY OF SCOTLAND

in association with
COLLINS
Fontana books

English—Matthew TEV—560P
BFBS/NBSS—1971—100M
ISBN 0 564 06531 5

© *American Bible Society, New York*
1966

Printed in Great Britain
Collins Clear-Type Press
London and Glasgow

THE GOSPEL OF MATTHEW

The Birth Record of Jesus Christ
(Also Luke 3.23–38)

1 This is the birth record of Jesus Christ, who was a descendant of David, who was a descendant of Abraham.

2 Abraham was the father of Isaac; Isaac was the father of Jacob; Jacob was the father of Judah and his brothers; 3 Judah was the father of Perez and Zerah (their mother was Tamar); Perez was the father of Hezron; Hezron was the father of Ram; 4 Ram was the father of Amminadab; Amminadab was the father of Nahshon; Nahshon was the father of Salmon; 5 Salmon was the father of Boaz (Rahab was his mother); Boaz was the father of Obed (Ruth was his mother); Obed was the father of Jesse; 6 Jesse was the father of King David.

David was the father of Solomon (his mother had been Uriah's wife); 7 Solomon was the father of Rehoboam; Rehoboam was the father of Abijah; Abijah was the father of Asa; 8 Asa was the father of Jehoshaphat; Jehoshaphat was the father of Joram; Joram was the father of Uzziah; 9 Uzziah was the father of Jotham; Jotham was the father of Ahaz; Ahaz was the father of Hezekiah; 10 Hezekiah was the father of Manasseh; Manasseh was the father of Amon; Amon was the father of Josiah; 11 Josiah was the father of Jechoniah and his brothers, at the time when the people of Israel were carried away to Babylon.

12 After the people were carried away to Babylon: Jechoniah was the father of Shealtiel; Shealtiel was the father of Zerubbabel; 13 Zerubbabel was the father of Abiud; Abiud was the father of Eliakim; Eliakim was the father of Azor; 14 Azor was the father of Zadok; Zadok was the father of Achim; Achim was the father of Eliud; 15 Eliud was the father of Eleazar; Eleazar was the father of Matthan; Matthan was the father of Jacob; 16 Jacob was the father of Joseph, the husband of Mary, who was the mother of Jesus, called the Messiah.

17 So then, there were fourteen sets of fathers and sons from Abraham to David, and fourteen from David to the time when the people were carried away to Babylon, and fourteen from then to the birth of the Messiah.

The Birth of Jesus Christ
(Also Luke 2.1–7)

¹⁸ This was the way that Jesus Christ was born. His mother Mary was engaged to Joseph, but before they were married she found out that she was going to have a baby by the Holy Spirit. ¹⁹ Joseph, to whom she was engaged, was a man who always did what was right; but he did not want to disgrace Mary publicly, so he made plans to break the engagement secretly. ²⁰ While he was thinking about all this, an angel of the Lord appeared to him in a dream and said: "Joseph, descendant of David, do not be afraid to take Mary to be your wife. For it is by the Holy Spirit that she has conceived. ²¹ She will give birth to a son and you will name him Jesus—for he will save his people from their sins."

²² Now all this happened in order to make come true what the Lord had said through the prophet: ²³ "The virgin will become pregnant and give birth to a son, and he will be called Emmanuel" (which means, "God is with us").

²⁴ So when Joseph woke up he did what the angel of the Lord had told him to do and married Mary. ²⁵ But he had no sexual relations with her before she gave birth to her son. And Joseph named him Jesus.

Visitors from the East

2 Jesus was born in the town of Bethlehem, in the land of Judea, during the time when Herod was king. Soon afterwards some men who studied the stars came from the east to Jerusalem ² and asked: "Where is the baby born to be the king of the Jews? We saw his star when it came up in the east, and we have come to worship him." ³ When King Herod heard about this he was very upset, and so was everybody else in Jerusalem. ⁴ He called together all the chief priests and the teachers of the Law and asked them, "Where will the Messiah be born?" ⁵ "In the town of Bethlehem, in Judea," they answered. "This is what the prophet wrote:

⁶ 'You, Bethlehem, in the land of Judah,
    Are not by any means the least among the
        rulers of Judah;
    For from you will come a leader
    Who will guide my people Israel.' "

⁷ So Herod called the visitors from the east to a secret

meeting and found out from them the exact time the star had appeared. ⁸ Then he sent them to Bethlehem with these instructions: "Go and make a careful search for the child, and when you find him let me know, so that I may go and worship him too." ⁹ With this they left, and on their way they saw the star — the same one they had seen in the east — and it went ahead of them until it came and stopped over the place where the child was. ¹⁰ How happy they were, what gladness they felt, when they saw the star! ¹¹ They went into the house and saw the child with his mother Mary. They knelt down and worshipped him; then they opened their bags and offered him presents: gold, frankincense, and myrrh.

¹² God warned them in a dream not to go back to Herod; so they went back home by another road.

The Escape to Egypt

¹³ After they had left, an angel of the Lord appeared in a dream to Joseph and said: "Get up, take the child and his mother and run away to Egypt, and stay there until I tell you to leave. Herod will be looking for the child to kill him." ¹⁴ So Joseph got up, took the child and his mother, and left during the night for Egypt, ¹⁵ where he stayed until Herod died.

This was done to make come true what the Lord had said through the prophet, "I called my Son out of Egypt."

The Killing of the Children

[16] When Herod realized that the visitors from the east had tricked him, he was furious. He gave orders to kill all the boys in Bethlehem and its neighbourhood who were two years old and younger — in accordance with what he had learned from the visitors about the time when the star had appeared.

[17] In this way what the prophet Jeremiah had said came true:

[18] "A sound is heard in Ramah,
The sound of bitter crying and weeping.
Rachel weeps for her children,
She weeps and will not be comforted,
Because they are all dead."

The Return from Egypt

[19] After Herod had died, an angel of the Lord appeared in a dream to Joseph, in Egypt, [20] and said: "Get up, take the child and his mother, and go back to the country of Israel, because those who tried to kill the child are dead." [21] So Joseph got up, took the child and his mother, and went back to the country of Israel.

[22] When he heard that Archelaus had succeeded his father Herod as king of Judea, Joseph was afraid to settle there. He was given more instructions in a dream, and so went to the province of Galilee [23] and made his home in a town named Nazareth. He did this to make come true what the prophets had said, "He will be called a Nazarene."

The Preaching of John the Baptist
(Also Mark 1.1–8; Luke 3.1–18; John 1.19–28)

3 At that time John the Baptist came and started preaching in the desert of Judea. [2] "Turn away from your sins," he said, "for the Kingdom of heaven is near!" [3] John was the one that the prophet Isaiah was talking about when he said:

"Someone is shouting in the desert:
'Get the Lord's road ready for him,
Make a straight path for him to travel!' "

4 John's clothes were made of camel's hair; he wore a leather belt around his waist, and ate locusts and wild honey. 5 People came to him from Jerusalem, from the whole province of Judea, and from all the country around the Jordan river. 6 They confessed their sins and he baptized them in the Jordan.

7 When John saw many Pharisees and Sadducees coming to him to be baptized, he said to them: "You snakes — who told you that you could escape from God's wrath that is about to come? 8 Do the things that will show that you have turned from your sins. 9 And do not think you can excuse yourselves by saying, 'Abraham is our ancestor.' I tell you that God can take these rocks and make descendants for Abraham! 10 The axe is ready to cut the trees at the roots; every tree that does not bear good fruit will be cut down and thrown in the fire. 11 I baptize you with water to show that you have repented; but the one who will come after me will baptize you with the Holy Spirit and fire. He is much greater than I am; I am not good enough even to carry his sandals. 12 He has his winnowing-shovel with him, to thresh out all the grain; he will gather his wheat into his barn, but burn the chaff in a fire that never goes out!"

The Baptism of Jesus
(Also Mark 1.9–11; Luke 3.21–22)

13 At that time Jesus went from Galilee to the Jordan, and came to John to be baptized by him. 14 But John tried to make him change his mind. "I ought to be baptized by you," John said, "yet you come to me!" 15 But Jesus answered him, "Let it be this way for now. For in this way we shall do all that God requires." So John agreed.

16 As soon as Jesus was baptized, he came up out of the water. Then heaven was opened to him, and he saw the Spirit of God coming down like a dove and lighting on him. 17 And then a voice said from heaven, "This is my own dear Son, with whom I am well pleased."

The Temptation of Jesus
(Also Mark 1.12–13; Luke 4.1–13)

4 Then the Spirit led Jesus into the desert to be tempted by the Devil. 2 After spending forty days and nights without food, Jesus was hungry. 3 The Devil came to him

and said, "If you are God's Son, order these stones to turn into bread." ⁴ Jesus answered, "The scripture says, 'Man cannot live on bread alone, but on every word that God speaks.' "

⁵ Then the Devil took Jesus to the Holy City, set him on the highest point of the Temple, ⁶ and said to him, "If you are God's Son, throw yourself down to the ground; for the scripture says,

'God will give orders to his angels about you:
They will hold you up with their hands,
So that you will not even hurt your feet on the
    stones.' "

⁷ Jesus answered, "But the scripture also says, 'You must not put the Lord your God to the test.' "

⁸ Then the Devil took Jesus to a very high mountain and showed him all the kingdoms of the world, in all their greatness. ⁹ "All this I will give you," the Devil said, "if you kneel down and worship me." ¹⁰ Then Jesus answered, "Go away, Satan! The scripture says, 'Worship the Lord your God and serve only him!' "

¹¹ So the Devil left him; and angels came and helped Jesus.

Jesus Begins His Work in Galilee
(Also Mark 1.14–15; Luke 4.14–15)

¹² When Jesus heard that John had been put in prison, he went away to Galilee. ¹³ He did not settle down in Nazareth, but went and lived in Capernaum, a town by Lake Galilee, in the territory of Zebulun and Naphtali. ¹⁴ This was done to make come true what the prophet Isaiah had said:

¹⁵ "Land of Zebulun, land of Naphtali,
In the direction of the sea, on the other side of
    Jordan,
Galilee of the Gentiles!
¹⁶ The people who live in darkness
Will see a great light!
On those who live in the dark land of death
The light will shine!"

¹⁷ From that time Jesus began to preach his message: "Turn away from your sins! The Kingdom of heaven is near!"

Jesus Calls Four Fishermen
(Also Mark 1.16–20; Luke 5.1–11)

¹⁸ As Jesus walked by Lake Galilee, he saw two brothers who were fishermen, Simon (called Peter) and his brother Andrew, catching fish in the lake with a net. ¹⁹ Jesus said to them, "Come with me and I will teach you to catch men." ²⁰ At once they left their nets and went with him.

²¹ He went on and saw two other brothers, James and John, the sons of Zebedee. They were in their boat with their father Zebedee, getting their nets ready. Jesus called them; ²² at once they left the boat and their father, and went with Jesus.

Jesus Teaches, Preaches, and Heals
(Also Luke 6.17–19)

²³ Jesus went all over Galilee, teaching in their synagogues, preaching the Good News of the Kingdom, and healing people from every kind of disease and sickness. ²⁴ The news about him spread through the whole country of Syria, so that people brought him all those who were sick with all kinds of diseases, and afflicted with all sorts

of troubles: people with demons, and epileptics, and paralytics — Jesus healed them all. [25] Great crowds followed him from Galilee and the Ten Towns, from Jerusalem, Judea, and the land on the other side of the Jordan.

The Sermon on the Mount

5 Jesus saw the crowds and went up a hill, where he sat down. His disciples gathered around him, [2] and he began to teach them:

True Happiness
(Also Luke 6.20–23)

[3] "Happy are those who know they are spiritually poor:
the Kingdom of heaven belongs to them!

[4] "Happy are those who mourn:
God will comfort them!

[5] "Happy are the meek:
they will receive what God has promised!

[6] "Happy are those whose greatest desire is to do what God requires:
God will satisfy them fully!

[7] "Happy are those who show mercy to others:
God will show mercy to them!

[8] "Happy are the pure in heart:
they will see God!

[9] "Happy are those who work for peace among men:
God will call them his sons!

¹⁰ "Happy are those who suffer persecution because they do what God requires:

the Kingdom of heaven belongs to them!

¹¹ "Happy are you when men insult you and mistreat you and tell all kinds of evil lies against you because you are my followers. ¹² Rejoice and be glad, because a great reward is kept for you in heaven. This is how men mistreated the prophets who lived before you."

Salt and Light
(Also Mark 9.50; Luke 14.34–35)

¹³ "You are like salt for all mankind. But if salt loses its taste, there is no way to make it salty again. It has become worthless; so it is thrown away and people walk on it.

¹⁴ "You are like the light for the world. A city built on a high hill cannot be hidden. ¹⁵ Nobody lights a lamp to put it under a bowl; instead he puts it on the lamp-stand, where it gives light for everyone in the house. ¹⁶ In the same way your light must shine before people, so that they will see the good things you do and give praise to your Father in heaven."

Teaching about the Law

¹⁷ "Do not think that I have come to do away with the Law of Moses and the teaching of the prophets. I have not come to do away with them, but to give them real meaning. ¹⁸ Remember this! As long as heaven and earth last, the least point or the smallest detail of the Law will not be done away with — not until the end of all things. ¹⁹ Therefore, whoever disobeys even the smallest of the commandments, and teaches others to do the same, will be least in the Kingdom of heaven. On the other hand, whoever obeys the Law, and teaches others to do the same, will be great in the Kingdom of heaven. ²⁰ I tell you, then, that you will be able to enter the Kingdom of heaven only if you are more faithful than the teachers of the Law and the Pharisees in doing what God requires."

Teaching about Anger

²¹ "You have heard that men were told in the past, 'Do not murder; anyone who commits murder will be brought before the judge.' ²² But now I tell you: whoever is angry

with his brother will be brought before the judge; whoever calls his brother 'You good-for-nothing!' will be brought before the Council; and whoever calls his brother a worthless fool will be in danger of going to the fire of hell. 23 So if you are about to offer your gift to God at the altar and there you remember that your brother has something against you, 24 leave your gift there in front of the altar and go at once to make peace with your brother; then come back and offer your gift to God.

25 "If a man brings a lawsuit against you and takes you to court, be friendly with him while there is time, before you get to court; once you are there he will turn you over to the judge, who will hand you over to the police, and you will be put in jail. 26 There you will stay, I tell you, until you pay the last penny of your fine."

Teaching about Adultery

27 "You have heard that it was said, 'Do not commit adultery.' 28 But now I tell you: anyone who looks at a woman and wants to possess her is guilty of committing adultery with her in his heart. 29 So if your right eye causes you to sin, take it out and throw it away! It is much better for you to lose a part of your body than to have your whole body thrown into hell. 30 If your right hand causes you to sin, cut it off and throw it away! It is much better for you to lose one of your limbs than to have your whole body go off to hell."

Teaching about Divorce
(Also Matt. 19.9; Mark 10.11-12; Luke 16.18)

31 "It was also said, 'Anyone who divorces his wife must give her a written notice of divorce.' 32 But now I tell you: if a man divorces his wife, and she has not been unfaithful, then he is guilty of making her commit adultery if she marries again; and the man who marries her also commits adultery."

Teaching about Vows

33 "You have also heard that men were told in the past, 'Do not break your promise, but do what you have sworn to do before the Lord.' 34 But now I tell you: do not use any vow when you make a promise; do not swear by heaven, because it is God's throne; 35 nor by earth, be-

cause it is the resting place for his feet; nor by Jerusalem, because it is the city of the great King. ³⁶ Do not even swear by your head, because you cannot make a single hair white or black. ³⁷ Just say 'Yes' or 'No' — anything else you have to say comes from the Evil One."

Teaching about Revenge
(*Also Luke 6.29–30*)

³⁸ "You have heard that it was said, 'An eye for an eye, and a tooth for a tooth.' ³⁹ But now I tell you: do not take revenge on someone who does you wrong. If anyone slaps you on the right cheek, let him slap your left cheek too. ⁴⁰ And if someone takes you to court to sue you for your shirt, let him have your coat as well. ⁴¹ And if one of the occupation troops forces you to carry his pack one mile, carry it another mile. ⁴² When someone asks you for

something, give it to him; when someone wants to borrow something, lend it to him."

Love for Enemies
(*Also Luke 6.27–28, 32–36*)

⁴³ "You have heard that it was said, 'Love your friends, hate your enemies.' ⁴⁴ But now I tell you: love your enemies, and pray for those who mistreat you, ⁴⁵ so that you will become the sons of your Father in heaven. For he makes his sun to shine on bad and good people alike, and

gives rain to those who do right and those who do wrong.
⁴⁶ Why should you expect God to reward you, if you love
only the people who love you? Even the tax collectors do
that! ⁴⁷ And if you speak only to your friends, have you
done anything out of the ordinary? Even the pagans do
that! ⁴⁸ You must be perfect — just as your Father in
heaven is perfect."

Teaching about Charity

6 "Be careful not to perform your religious duties in
public so that people will see what you do. If you do
these things publicly you will not have any reward from
your Father in heaven.

² "So when you give something to a needy person, do
not make a big show of it, as the show-offs do in the synagogues and on the streets. They do it so that people
will praise them. Remember this! They have already been
paid in full. ³ But when you help a needy person, do it in
such a way that even your closest friend will not know
about it, ⁴ but it will be a private matter. And your Father,
who sees what you do in private, will reward you."

Teaching about Prayer
(Also Luke 11.2–4)

⁵ "And when you pray, do not be like the show-offs!
They love to stand up and pray in the synagogues and
on the street corners so that everybody will see them. Remember this! They have already been paid in full. ⁶ But
when you pray, go to your room and close the door, and
pray to your Father, who is unseen. And your Father, who
sees what you do in private, will reward you.

⁷ "In your prayers do not use a lot of words, as the
pagans do, who think that God will hear them because of
their long prayers. ⁸ Do not be like them; your Father
already knows what you need before you ask him. ⁹ This is
the way you should pray:
'Our Father in heaven:
    May your name be kept holy,
¹⁰ May your Kingdom come,
    May your will be done on earth as it is in heaven.
¹¹ Give us today the food we need;
¹² Forgive us the wrongs that we have done,
    As we forgive the wrongs that others have done us;

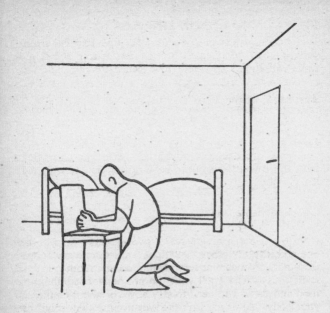

¹³ Do not bring us to hard testing, but keep us safe from
  the Evil One.'
¹⁴ For if you forgive others the wrongs they have done
you, your Father in heaven will also forgive you. ¹⁵ But if
you do not forgive the wrongs of others, then your Father
in heaven will not forgive the wrongs you have done."

Teaching about Fasting

¹⁶ "And when you fast, do not put on a sad face like the
show-offs do. They go around with a hungry look so that
everybody will be sure to see that they are fasting. Remember this! They have already been paid in full.
¹⁷ When you go without food, wash your face and comb
your hair, ¹⁸ so that others cannot know that you are fasting
— only your Father, who is unseen, will know. And your
Father, who sees what you do in private, will reward you."

Riches in Heaven
(Also Luke 12.33–34)

¹⁹ "Do not save riches here on earth, where moths and
rust destroy, and robbers break in and steal. ²⁰ Instead,

save riches in heaven, where moths and rust cannot destroy, and robbers cannot break in and steal. 21 For your heart will always be where your riches are."

The Light of the Body
(Also Luke 11.34-36)

22 "The eyes are like a lamp for the body: if your eyes are clear, your whole body will be full of light; 23 but if your eyes are bad, your body will be in darkness. So if the light in you turns out to be darkness, how terribly dark it will be!"

God and Possessions
(Also Luke 16.13; 12.22-31)

24 "No one can be a slave to two masters: he will hate one and love the other; he will be loyal to one and despise the other. You cannot serve both God and money.

25 "This is why I tell you: do not be worried about the food and drink you need to stay alive, or about clothes for your body. After all, isn't life worth more than food? and isn't the body worth more than clothes? 26 Look at the birds flying around: they do not plant seeds, gather a harvest, and put it in barns; your Father in heaven takes care of them! Aren't you worth much more than birds? 27 Which one of you can live a few years more by worrying about it?

28 "And why worry about clothes? Look how the wild flowers grow: they do not work or make clothes for themselves. 29 But I tell you that not even Solomon, as rich as he was, had clothes as beautiful as one of these flowers. 30 It is God who clothes the wild grass — grass that is here today, gone tomorrow, burned up in the oven. Will he not be all the more sure to clothe you? How little is your faith! 31 So do not start worrying: 'Where will my food come from? or my drink? or my clothes?' 32 (These are the things the heathen are always after.) Your Father in heaven knows that you need all these things. 33 Instead, give first place to his Kingdom and to what he requires, and he will provide you with all these other things. 34 So do not worry about tomorrow; it will have enough worries of its own. There is no need to add to the troubles each day brings."

Judging Others
(*Also Luke 6.37–38, 41–42*)

7 "Do not judge others, so that God will not judge you — ² because God will judge you in the same way you judge others, and he will apply to you the same rules you apply to others. ³ Why, then, do you look at the speck in your brother's eye, and pay no attention to the log in your own eye? ⁴ How dare you say to your brother, 'Please, let me take that speck out of your eye,' when you have a log in your own eye? ⁵ You impostor! Take the log out of your own eye first, and then you will be able to see and take the speck out of your brother's eye.

⁶ "Do not give what is holy to dogs — they will only turn and attack you; do not throw your pearls in front of pigs — they will only trample them underfoot."

Ask, Seek, Knock
(*Also Luke 11.9–13*)

⁷ "Ask, and you will receive; seek, and you will find; knock, and the door will be opened to you. ⁸ For everyone who asks will receive, and he who seeks will find, and the door will be opened to him who knocks. ⁹ Would any one of you fathers give his son a stone, when he asks you for bread? ¹⁰ Or would you give him a snake, when he asks you for fish? ¹¹ As bad as you are, you know how to give good things to your children. How much more, then, your Father in heaven will give good things to those who ask him!

¹² "Do for others what you want them to do for you: this is the meaning of the Law of Moses and the teaching of the prophets."

The Narrow Gate
(*Also Luke 13.24*)

¹³ "Go in through the narrow gate, for the gate is wide and the road is easy that leads to hell, and there are many who travel it. ¹⁴ The gate is narrow and the way is hard that leads to life, and few people find it."

A Tree and Its Fruit
(*Also Luke 6.43–44*)

¹⁵ "Watch out for false prophets; they come to you looking like sheep on the outside, but they are really like wild

wolves on the inside. ¹⁶ You will know them by the way
they act. Thorn bushes do not bear grapes, and briars do
not bear figs. ¹⁷ A healthy tree bears good fruit, while a
poor tree bears bad fruit. ¹⁸ A healthy tree cannot bear
bad fruit, and a poor tree cannot bear good fruit. ¹⁹ Any
tree that does not bear good fruit is cut down and thrown
in the fire. ²⁰ So, then, you will know the false prophets
by the way they act."

I Never Knew You
(Also Luke 13.25–27)

²¹ "Not every person who calls me 'Lord, Lord,' will enter into the Kingdom of heaven, but only those who do
what my Father in heaven wants them to do. ²² When that
Day comes, many will say to me, 'Lord, Lord! In your
name we told God's message, by your name we drove out
many demons and performed many miracles!' ²³ Then I
will say to them, 'I never knew you. Away from me, you
evildoers!' "

The Two House Builders
(Also Luke 6.47–49)

²⁴ "So then, everyone who hears these words of mine
and obeys them will be like a wise man who built his
house on the rock. ²⁵ The rain poured down, the rivers
flooded over, and the winds blew hard against that house.
But it did not fall, because it had been built on the rock.
²⁶ Everyone who hears these words of mine and does not
obey them will be like a foolish man who built his house
on the sand. ²⁷ The rain poured down, the rivers flooded
over, the winds blew hard against that house, and it fell.
What a terrible fall that was!"

The Authority of Jesus

²⁸ Jesus finished saying these things, and the crowds
were amazed at the way he taught. ²⁹ He wasn't like their
teachers of the Law; instead, he taught with authority.

Jesus Makes a Leper Clean
(Also Mark 1.40–45; Luke 5.12–16)

8 Jesus came down from the hill, and large crowds followed him. ² Then a leper came to him, knelt down
before him, and said, "Sir, if you want to, you can make

me clean." ³ Jesus reached out and touched him. "I do want to," he answered. "Be clean!" At once he was clean from his leprosy. ⁴ Then Jesus said to him: "Listen! Don't tell anyone, but go straight to the priest and let him examine you; then offer the sacrifice that Moses ordered, to prove to everyone that you are now clean."

Jesus Heals a Roman Officer's Servant
(Also Luke 7.1–10)

⁵ When Jesus entered Capernaum, a Roman officer met him and begged for help: ⁶ "Sir, my servant is home, sick in bed, unable to move, and suffering terribly." ⁷ "I will go and make him well," Jesus said. ⁸ "Oh no, sir," answered the officer. "I do not deserve to have you come into my house. Just give the order and my servant will get well. ⁹ I, too, am a man with superior officers over me, and I have soldiers under me; so I order this one, 'Go!' and he goes; and I order that one, 'Come!' and he comes; and I order my slave, 'Do this!' and he does it." ¹⁰ Jesus was surprised when he heard this, and said to the people who were following him: "I tell you, I have never seen such faith as this in anyone in Israel. ¹¹ Remember this! Many will come from the east and the west and sit down at the table in the Kingdom of heaven with Abraham, Isaac, and Jacob. ¹² But those who should be in the Kingdom will be thrown out into the darkness outside, where they will cry and gnash their teeth." ¹³ And Jesus said to the officer, "Go home, and what you believe will be done for you." And the officer's servant was healed that very hour.

Jesus Heals Many People
(Also Mark 1.29–34; Luke 4.38–41)

¹⁴ Jesus went to Peter's home, and there he saw Peter's mother-in-law sick in bed with a fever. ¹⁵ He touched her hand; the fever left her, and she got up and began to wait on him.

¹⁶ When evening came, people brought to Jesus many who had demons in them. Jesus drove out the evil spirits with a word and healed all who were sick. ¹⁷ He did this to make come true what the prophet Isaiah had said, "He himself took our illnesses and carried away our diseases."

The Would-Be Followers of Jesus
(Also Luke 9.57–62)

¹⁸ Jesus noticed the crowd around him and gave orders to go to the other side of the lake. ¹⁹ A teacher of the Law came to him. "Teacher," he said, "I am ready to go with you wherever you go." ²⁰ Jesus answered him, "Foxes have holes, and birds have nests, but the Son of Man has no place to lie down and rest." ²¹ Another man, who was a disciple, said, "Sir, first let me go and bury my father." ²² "Follow me," Jesus answered, "and let the dead bury their own dead."

Jesus Calms a Storm
(Also Mark 4.35–41; Luke 8.22–25)

²³ Jesus got into the boat, and his disciples went with him. ²⁴ Suddenly a fierce storm hit the lake, so that the waves covered the boat. But Jesus was asleep. ²⁵ The disciples went to him and woke him up. "Save us, Lord!" they said. "We are about to die!" ²⁶ "Why are you so frightened?" Jesus answered. "How little faith you have!" Then he got up and gave a command to the winds and to the waves, and there was a great calm. ²⁷ Everyone was amazed. "What kind of man is this?" they said. "Even the winds and the waves obey him!"

Jesus Heals Two Men with Demons
(Also Mark 5.1–20; Luke 8.26–39)

²⁸ Jesus came to the territory of the Gadarenes, on the other side of the lake, and was met by two men who came out of the burial caves. These men had demons in them and were very fierce, so dangerous that no one dared travel on that road. ²⁹ At once they screamed, "What do you want with us, Son of God? Have you come to punish us before the right time?" ³⁰ Not far away a large herd of pigs was feeding. ³¹ The demons begged Jesus, "If you are going to drive us out, send us into that herd of pigs." ³² "Go," Jesus told them; so they left and went off into the pigs. The whole herd rushed down the side of the cliff into the lake and were drowned.

³³ The men who had been taking care of the pigs ran away and went to the town, where they told the whole story, and what had happened to the men with the demons. ³⁴ So everybody from that town went out to meet Jesus;

and when they saw him they begged him to leave their territory.

Jesus Heals a Paralyzed Man
(Also Mark 2.1–12; Luke 5.17–26)

9 Jesus got into the boat, went back across the lake, and came to his own town. ² Some people brought him a paralyzed man, lying on a bed. Jesus saw how much faith they had, and said to the paralyzed man, "Courage, my son! Your sins are forgiven." ³ Then some teachers of the Law said to themselves, "This man is talking against God!" ⁴ Jesus knew what they were thinking and said: "Why are you thinking such evil things? ⁵ Is it easier to say, 'Your sins are forgiven,' or to say, 'Get up and walk'? ⁶ I will prove to you, then, that the Son of Man has authority on earth to forgive sins." So he said to the paralyzed man, "Get up, pick up your bed, and go home!" ⁷ The man got up and went home. ⁸ When the people saw it, they were afraid, and praised God for giving such authority as this to men.

Jesus Calls Matthew
(Also Mark 2.13–17; Luke 5.27–32)

⁹ Jesus left that place, and as he walked along he saw a tax collector, named Matthew, sitting in his office. He said to him, "Follow me." And Matthew got up and followed him.

¹⁰ While Jesus was having dinner at his house, many tax collectors and outcasts came and joined him and his disciples at the table. ¹¹ Some Pharisees saw this and said to his disciples, "Why does your teacher eat with tax collectors and outcasts?" ¹² Jesus heard them and answered: "People who are well do not need a doctor, but only those who are sick. ¹³ Go and find out what this scripture means, 'I do not want animal sacrifices, but kindness.' For I have not come to call the respectable people, but the outcasts."

The Question about Fasting
(Also Mark 2.18–22; Luke 5.33–39)

¹⁴ Then the followers of John the Baptist came to Jesus, asking, "Why is it that we and the Pharisees fast often, but your disciples don't fast at all?" ¹⁵ Jesus answered: "Do you expect the guests at a wedding party to be sad as

long as the bridegroom is with them? Of course not! But the time will come when the bridegroom will be taken away from them, and then they will go without food.

[16] "No one patches up an old coat with a piece of new cloth; for such a patch tears off from the coat, making an even bigger hole. [17] Nor does anyone pour new wine into used wineskins. If he does, the skins will burst, and then the wine pours out and the skins will be ruined. Instead, new wine is poured into fresh wineskins, and both will keep in good condition."

The Official's Daughter and the Woman who Touched Jesus' Cloak
(Also Mark 5.21–43; Luke 8.40–56)

[18] While Jesus was saying this to them, a Jewish official came to him, knelt down before him, and said, "My daughter has just died; but come and place your hand on her and she will live." [19] So Jesus got up and followed him, and his disciples went with him.

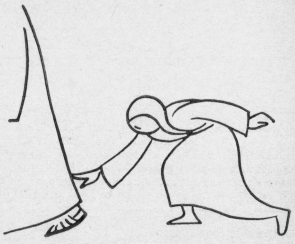

[20] A certain woman, who had had severe bleeding for twelve years, came up behind Jesus and touched the edge of his cloak. [21] She said to herself, "If only I touch his cloak I will get well." [22] Jesus turned round and saw her, and said, "Courage, my daughter! Your faith has made

you well." At that very moment the woman became well.

²³ So Jesus went into the official's house. When he saw the musicians for the funeral, and the people all stirred up, ²⁴ he said, "Get out, everybody! The little girl is not dead — she is just sleeping!" They all started making fun of him. ²⁵ As soon as the people had been put out, Jesus went into the girl's room and took hold of her hand, and she got up. ²⁶ The news about this spread all over that part of the country.

Jesus Heals Two Blind Men

²⁷ Jesus left that place, and as he walked along two blind men started following him. "Have mercy on us, Son of David!" they shouted. ²⁸ When Jesus had gone indoors, the two blind men came to him and he asked them, "Do you believe that I can do this?" "Yes, sir!" they answered. ²⁹ Then Jesus touched their eyes and said, "May it happen, then, just as you believe!" — ³⁰ and their sight was restored. Jesus spoke harshly to them, "Don't tell this to anyone!" ³¹ But they left and spread the news about Jesus all over that part of the country.

Jesus Heals a Dumb Man

³² As the men were leaving, some people brought to Jesus a man who could not talk because he had a demon. ³³ As soon as the demon was driven out, the man started talking. Everybody was amazed. "We never saw the like in Israel!" they exclaimed. ³⁴ But the Pharisees said, "It is the chief of the demons who gives him the power to drive them out."

Jesus Has Pity for the People

³⁵ So Jesus went round visiting all the towns and villages. He taught in their synagogues, preached the Good News of the Kingdom, and healed people from every kind of disease and sickness. ³⁶ As he saw the crowds, his heart was filled with pity for them, because they were worried and helpless, like sheep without a shepherd. ³⁷ So he said to his disciples, "There is a great harvest, but few workers to gather it in. ³⁸ Pray to the owner of the harvest that he will send out more workers to gather in his harvest."

The Twelve Apostles
(Also Mark 3.13–19; Luke 6.12–16)

10 Jesus called his twelve disciples together and gave them authority to drive out the evil spirits and to heal every disease and every sickness. [2] These are the names of the twelve apostles: first, Simon (called Peter) and his brother Andrew; James and his brother John, the sons of Zebedee; [3] Philip and Bartholomew; Thomas and Matthew, the tax collector; James, the son of Alphaeus, and Thaddaeus; [4] Simon, the patriot, and Judas Iscariot, who betrayed Jesus.

The Mission of the Twelve
(Also Mark 6.7–13; Luke 9.1–6)

[5] Jesus sent these twelve men out with the following instructions: "Do not go to any Gentile territory or any Samaritan towns. [6] Go, instead, to the lost sheep of the people of Israel. [7] Go and preach, 'The Kingdom of heaven is near!' [8] Heal the sick, raise the dead, make the lepers clean, drive out demons. You have received without paying, so give without being paid. [9] Do not carry any gold, silver, or copper money in your pockets; [10] do not carry a beggar's bag for the trip, or an extra shirt, or shoes, or a walking stick. A worker should be given what he needs.

[11] "When you come to a town or village, go in and look for someone who is willing to welcome you, and stay with him until you leave that place. [12] When you go into a house say, 'Peace be with you.' [13] If the people in that house welcome you, let your greeting of peace remain; but if they do not welcome you, then take back your greeting. [14] And if some home or town will not welcome you or listen to you, then leave that place and shake the dust off your feet. [15] Remember this! On the Judgment Day God will show more mercy to the people of Sodom and Gomorrah than to the people of that town!"

Coming Persecutions
(Also Mark 13.9–13; Luke 21.12–17)

[16] "Listen! I am sending you just like sheep to a pack of wolves. You must be as cautious as snakes and as gentle as doves. [17] Watch out, for there will be men who

will arrest you and take you to court, and they will whip you in their synagogues. ¹⁸ You will be brought to trial before rulers and kings for my sake, to tell the Good News to them and to the Gentiles. ¹⁹ When they bring you to trial, do not worry about what you are going to say or how you will say it; when the time comes, you will be given what you will say. ²⁰ For the words you speak will not be yours; they will come from the Spirit of your Father speaking in you.

²¹ "Men will hand over their own brothers to be put to death, and fathers will do the same to their children; children will turn against their parents and have them put to death. ²² Everyone will hate you, because of me. But the person who holds out to the end will be saved. ²³ And when they persecute you in one town, run away to another one. I tell you, you will not finish your work in all the towns of Israel before the Son of Man comes.

²⁴ "No pupil is greater than his teacher; no slave is greater than his master. ²⁵ So a pupil should be satisfied to become like his teacher, and a slave like his master. If the head of the family is called Beelzebul, the members of the family will be called by even worse names!"

Whom to Fear
(Also Luke 12.2–7)

²⁶ "Do not be afraid of men, then. Whatever is covered up will be uncovered, and every secret will be made known. ²⁷ What I am telling you in the dark you must repeat in broad daylight, and what you have heard in private you must tell from the housetops. ²⁸ Do not be afraid of those who kill the body but cannot kill the soul; rather be afraid of God, who can destroy both body and soul in hell. ²⁹ You can buy two sparrows for a penny; yet not a single one of them falls to the ground without your Father's consent. ³⁰ As for you, even the hairs of your head have all been counted. ³¹ So do not be afraid: you are worth much more than sparrows!"

Confessing and Denying Christ
(Also Luke 12.8–9)

³² "Whoever declares publicly that he belongs to me, I will do the same for him before my Father in heaven.

33 But whoever denies publicly that he belongs to me, then I will deny him before my Father in heaven."

Not Peace, but a Sword
(Also Luke 12.51–53; 14.26–27)

34 "Do not think that I have come to bring peace to the world; no, I did not come to bring peace, but a sword. 35 I came to set sons against their fathers, daughters against their mothers, daughters-in-law against their mothers-in-law; 36 a man's worst enemies will be the members of his own family.

37 "Whoever loves his father or mother more than me is not worthy of me; whoever loves his son or daughter more than me is not worthy of me. 38 Whoever does not take up his cross and follow in my steps is not worthy of me. 39 Whoever tries to gain his own life will lose it; whoever loses his life for my sake will gain it."

Rewards
(Also Mark 9.41)

40 "Whoever welcomes you, welcomes me; and whoever welcomes me, welcomes the one who sent me. 41 Whoever welcomes God's messenger because he is God's messenger will share in his reward; and whoever welcomes a truly good man, because he is that, will share in his reward. 42 And remember this! Whoever gives even a drink of cold water to one of the least of these my followers, because he is my follower, will certainly receive his reward."

The Messengers from John the Baptist
(Also Luke 7.18–35)

11 When Jesus finished giving these instructions to his twelve disciples, he left that place and went on to teach and preach in the towns near there.

2 When John the Baptist heard in prison about Christ's works, he sent some of his disciples to him. 3 "Tell us," they asked Jesus, "are you the one John said was going to come, or should we expect someone else?" 4 Jesus answered: "Go back and tell John what you are hearing and seeing: 5 the blind can see, the lame can walk, the lepers are made clean, the deaf hear, the dead are raised to life, and the Good News is preached to the poor. 6 How happy is he who has no doubts about me!"

7 While John's disciples were going back, Jesus spoke about John to the crowds. "When you went out to John in the desert, what did you expect to see? A blade of grass bending in the wind? 8 What did you go out to see? A man dressed up in fancy clothes? People who dress like that live in palaces! 9 Tell me, what did you expect to see? A prophet? Yes, I tell you — you saw much more than a prophet. 10 For John is the one of whom the scripture says: 'Here is my messenger, says God; I will send him ahead of you to open the way for you.' 11 Remember this! John the Baptist is greater than any man who has ever lived. But he who is least in the Kingdom of heaven is greater than he. 12 From the time John preached his message until this very day the Kingdom of heaven has suffered violent attacks, and violent men try to seize it. 13 All the prophets and the Law of Moses, until the time of John, spoke about the Kingdom; 14 and if you are willing to believe their message, John is Elijah, whose coming was predicted. 15 Listen, then, if you have ears!

16 "Now, to what can I compare the people of this day? They are like children sitting in the market place. One group shouts to the other, 17 'We played wedding music for you, but you would not dance! We sang funeral songs, but you would not cry!' 18 John came, and he fasted and drank no wine, and everyone said, 'He is a madman!' 19 The Son of Man came, and he ate and drank, and everyone said, 'Look at this man! He is a glutton and wine-drinker, and is a friend of tax collectors and out-

casts!' God's wisdom, however, is shown to be true by its results."

The Unbelieving Towns
(Also Luke 10.13–15)

20 Then Jesus began to reproach the towns where he had performed most of his miracles, because the people had not turned from their sins. 21 "How terrible it will be for you, Chorazin! How terrible for you too, Bethsaida! For if the miracles which were performed in you had been performed in Tyre and Sidon, long ago the people there would have put on sackcloth, and sprinkled ashes on themselves to show they had turned from their sins! 22 Remember, then, that on the Judgment Day God will show more mercy to the people of Tyre and Sidon than to you! 23 And as for you, Capernaum! You wanted to lift yourself up to heaven? You will be thrown down to hell! For if the miracles which were performed in you had been performed in Sodom, it would still be in existence today! 24 Remember, then, that on the Judgment Day God will show more mercy to Sodom than to you!"

Come to Me and Rest
(Also Luke 10.21–22)

25 At that time Jesus said: "O Father, Lord of heaven

and earth! I thank you because you have shown to the
unlearned what you have hidden from the wise and
learned. ²⁶ Yes, Father, this was done by your own choice
and pleasure.

²⁷ "My Father has given me all things. No one knows
the Son except the Father, and no one knows the Father
except the Son, and those to whom the Son wants to reveal
him.

²⁸ "Come to me, all of you who are tired from carrying
your heavy loads, and I will give you rest. ²⁹ Take my
yoke and put it on you, and learn from me, for I am gentle
and humble in spirit; and you will find rest. ³⁰ The yoke
I will give you is easy, and the load I will put on you is
light."

The Question about the Sabbath
(Also Mark 2.23–28; Luke 6.1–5)

12 Not long afterward Jesus was walking through the
wheat fields on a Sabbath day. His disciples were
hungry, so they began to pick heads of wheat and eat the
grain. ² When the Pharisees saw this, they said to Jesus,
"Look, it is against our Law for your disciples to do this
on the Sabbath!" ³ Jesus answered: "Have you never read
what David did that time when he and his men were
hungry? ⁴ He went into the house of God, and he and
his men ate the bread offered to God, even though it was
against the Law for them to eat that bread — only the
priests were allowed to eat it. ⁵ Or have you not read in
the Law of Moses that every Sabbath the priests in the
Temple actually break the Sabbath law, yet they are not
guilty? ⁶ There is something here, I tell you, greater than
the Temple. ⁷ If you really knew what this scripture means,
'I do not want animal sacrifices, but kindness,' you would
not condemn people who are not guilty. ⁸ For the Son of
Man is Lord of the Sabbath."

The Man with a Crippled Hand
(Also Mark 3.1–6; Luke 6.6–11)

⁹ Jesus left that place and went to one of their syna-
gogues. ¹⁰ A man was there who had a crippled hand.
There were some men present who wanted to accuse
Jesus of wrongdoing; so they asked him, "Is it against our
Law to cure on the Sabbath?" ¹¹ Jesus answered: "What

if one of you has a sheep and it falls into a deep hole on the Sabbath? Will you not take hold of it and lift it out? 12 And a man is worth much more than a sheep! So, then, our Law does allow us to help someone on the Sabbath." 13 Then he said to the man, "Stretch out your hand." He stretched it out, and it became well again, just like the other one. 14 The Pharisees left and made plans against Jesus to kill him.

God's Chosen Servant

15 When Jesus heard about it, he went away from that place; and many people followed him. He healed all the sick, 16 and gave them orders not to tell others about him, 17 to make come true what the prophet Isaiah had said:
18 "Here is my servant, says God, whom I have
      chosen,
   The one I love, with whom I am well pleased.
   I will put my Spirit on him,
   And he will announce my judgment to all
      people.
19 But he will not argue or shout,
   Nor will he make loud speeches in the streets;
20 He will not break off a bent reed,
   Nor will he put out a flickering lamp.
   He will persist until he causes justice to tri-
      umph;
21 And all people will put their hope in him."

Jesus and Beelzebul
(Also Mark 3.20–30; Luke 11.14–23)

22 Then some people brought to Jesus a man who was blind and could not talk because he had a demon. Jesus healed the man, so that he was able to talk and see. 23 The crowds were all amazed. "Could he be the Son of David?" they asked. 24 When the Pharisees heard this they replied, "He drives out demons only because their ruler Beelzebul gives him power to do so." 25 Jesus knew what they were thinking and said to them: "Any country that divides itself into groups that fight each other will not last very long. And any town or family that divides itself into groups that fight each other will fall apart. 26 So if one group is fighting another in Satan's kingdom, this means that it is already divided into groups and will soon fall apart! 27 You

say that I drive out demons because Beelzebul gives me the power to do so. Well, then, who gives your followers the power to drive them out? Your own followers prove that you are completely wrong! 28 No, it is God's Spirit who gives me the power to drive out demons, which proves that the Kingdom of God has already come upon you.

29 "No one can break into a strong man's house and take away his belongings unless he ties up the strong man first; then he can plunder his house.

30 "Anyone who is not for me is really against me; anyone who does not help me gather is really scattering. 31 For this reason I tell you: men can be forgiven any sin and any evil thing they say; but whoever says evil things against the Holy Spirit will not be forgiven. 32 Anyone who says something against the Son of Man will be forgiven; but whoever says something against the Holy Spirit will not be forgiven — now or ever."

A Tree and Its Fruit
(Also Luke 6.43–45)

33 "To have good fruit you must have a healthy tree; if you have a poor tree you will have bad fruit. For a tree is known by the kind of fruit it bears. 34 You snakes — how can you say good things when you are evil? For the mouth speaks what the heart is full of. 35 A good man brings good things out of his treasure of good things; a bad man brings bad things out of his treasure of bad things.

36 "And I tell you this: on the Judgment Day everyone will have to give account of every useless word he has ever spoken. 37 For your words will be used to judge you, either to declare you innocent or to declare you guilty."

The Demand for a Miracle
(Also Mark 8.11–12; Luke 11.29–32)

38 Then some teachers of the Law and some Pharisees spoke up. "Teacher," they said, "we want to see you perform a miracle." 39 "How evil and godless are the people of this day!" Jesus exclaimed. "You ask me for a miracle? No! The only miracle you will be given is the miracle of the prophet Jonah. 40 In the same way that Jonah spent three days and nights in the belly of the big fish, so will the Son of Man spend three days and nights in the depths of the earth. 41 On the Judgment Day the people of

Nineveh will stand up and accuse you, because they turned from their sins when they heard Jonah preach; and there is something here, I tell you, greater than Jonah! 42 On the Judgment Day the Queen from the South will stand up and accuse you, because she travelled halfway round the world to listen to Solomon's wise teaching; and there is something here, I tell you, greater than Solomon!"

The Return of the Evil Spirit
(Also Luke 11.24–26)

43 "When an evil spirit goes out of a man, it travels over dry country looking for a place to rest. If it can't find one, 44 it says to itself, 'I will go back to my house which I left.' So it goes back and finds it empty, clean, and all fixed up. 45 Then it goes out and brings along seven other spirits even worse than itself, and they come and live there. So that man is in worse shape, when it is all over, than he was at the beginning. This is the way it will happen to the evil people of this day."

Jesus' Mother and Brothers
(Also Mark 3.31–35; Luke 8.19–21)

46 Jesus was still talking to the people when his mother and brothers arrived. They stood outside, asking to speak with him. 47 So one of the people there said to him, "Look, your mother and brothers are standing outside, and they want to speak with you." 48 Jesus answered, "Who is my mother? Who are my brothers?" 49 Then he pointed to his disciples and said: "Look! Here are my mother and my brothers! 50 For the person who does what my Father in heaven wants him to do is my brother, my sister, my mother."

The Parable of the Sower
(Also Mark 4.1–9; Luke 8.4–8)

13 That same day Jesus left the house and went to the lakeside, where he sat down to teach. 2 The crowd that gathered around him was so large that he got into a boat and sat in it, while the crowd stood on the shore. 3 He used parables to tell them many things.

"There was a man who went out to sow. 4 As he scattered the seed in the field, some of it fell along the path, and the birds came and ate it up. 5 Some of it fell on rocky ground, where there was little soil. The seeds soon sprouted, because the soil wasn't deep. 6 When the sun came up it burned the young plants, and because the roots had not grown deep enough the plants soon dried up. 7 Some of the seed fell among thorns, which grew up and choked the plants. 8 But some seeds fell in good soil, and bore grain: some had one hundred grains, others sixty, and others thirty." 9 And Jesus said, "Listen, then, if you have ears!"

The Purpose of the Parables
(Also Mark 4.10–12; Luke 8.9–10)

10 Then the disciples came to Jesus and asked him, "Why do you use parables when you talk to them?" 11 "The knowledge of the secrets of the Kingdom of heaven has been given to you," Jesus answered, "but not to them. 12 For the man who has something will be given more, so that he will have more than enough; but the man who has nothing will have taken away from him even the little he has. 13 This is the reason that I use parables to talk to them: it is because they look, but do not see, and they listen, but do not hear or understand. 14 So the prophecy of Isaiah comes true in their case:

'You will listen and listen, but not understand;
You will look and look, but not see.
15 Because this people's mind is dull;
They have stopped up their ears,
And they have closed their eyes.
Otherwise, their eyes might see,
Their ears might hear,
Their minds might understand
And they might turn to me, says God,
And I would heal them.'

16 As for you, how fortunate you are! Your eyes see and your ears hear. 17 Remember this! Many prophets and many of God's people wanted very much to see what you see, but they could not, and to hear what you hear, but they did not."

Jesus Explains the Parable of the Sower
(Also Mark 4.13–20; Luke 8.11–15)

18 "Listen, then, and learn what the parable of the sower means. 19 Those who hear the message about the King-

dom but do not understand it are like the seed that fell
along the path. The Evil One comes and snatches away
what was sown in them. 20 The seed that fell on rocky
ground stands for those who receive the message gladly
as soon as they hear it. 21 But it does not sink deep in
them, and they don't last long. So when trouble or perse-
cution comes because of the message, they give up at
once. 22 The seed that fell among thorns stands for those
who hear the message, but the worries about this life and
the love for riches choke the message, and they don't bear
fruit. 23 And the seed sown in the good soil stands for
those who hear the message and understand it: they bear
fruit, some as much as one hundred, others sixty, and
others thirty."

The Parable of the Weeds

24 Jesus told them another parable: "The Kingdom of
heaven is like a man who sowed good seed in his field.
25 One night, when everyone was asleep, an enemy came
and sowed weeds among the wheat, and went away.
26 When the plants grew and the heads of grain began to
form, then the weeds showed up. 27 The man's servants
came to him and said, 'Sir, it was good seed you sowed
in your field; where did the weeds come from?' 28 'It was
some enemy who did this,' he answered. 'Do you want us
to go and pull up the weeds?' they asked him. 29 'No,' he
answered, 'because as you gather the weeds you might pull
up some of the wheat along with them. 30 Let the wheat
and the weeds both grow together until harvest, and then
I will tell the harvest workers: Pull up the weeds first and
tie them in bundles to throw in the fire; then gather in the
wheat and put it in my barn.' "

The Parable of the Mustard Seed
(Also Mark 4.30–32; Luke 13.18–19)

31 Jesus told them another parable: "The Kingdom of
heaven is like a mustard seed, the smallest of all seeds; 32 a
man takes it and sows it in his field, and when it grows up
it is the biggest of all plants. It becomes a tree, so that the
birds come and make their nests in its branches."

The Parable of the Yeast
(Also Luke 13.20–21)

33 Jesus told them another parable: "The Kingdom of heaven is like yeast. A woman takes it and mixes it with a bushel of flour, until the whole batch of dough rises."

Jesus' Use of Parables
(Also Mark 4.33–34)

34 Jesus used parables to tell all these things to the crowds; he would not say a thing to them without using a parable. 35 He did this to make come true what the prophet had said:

"I will use parables when I speak to them,
I will tell them things unknown since the creation of the world."

Jesus Explains the Parable of the Weeds

36 Then Jesus left the crowd and went indoors. His disciples came to him and said, "Tell us what the parable of the weeds in the field means." 37 Jesus answered: "The man who sowed the good seed is the Son of Man; 38 the field is the world; the good seed is the people who belong to the Kingdom; the weeds are the people who belong to the Evil One; 39 and the enemy who sowed the weeds is the Devil himself. The harvest is the end of the age, and the harvest workers are angels. 40 Just as the weeds are gathered up and burned in the fire, so it will be at the end of the age: 41 the Son of Man will send out his angels and they will gather up out of his Kingdom all who cause people to sin, and all other evildoers, 42 and throw them into the fiery furnace, where they will cry and gnash their teeth. 43 Then God's people will shine like the sun in their Father's Kingdom. Listen, then, if you have ears!"

The Parable of the Hidden Treasure

44 "The Kingdom of heaven is like a treasure hidden in a field. A man happens to find it, so he covers it up again. He is so happy that he goes and sells everything he has, and then goes back and buys the field."

The Parable of the Pearl

45 "Also, the Kingdom of heaven is like a buyer looking for fine pearls. 46 When he finds one that is unusually

fine, he goes and sells everything he has, and buys the pearl."

The Parable of the Net

⁴⁷ "Also, the Kingdom of heaven is like a net thrown out in the lake, which catches all kinds of fish. ⁴⁸ When it is full, the fishermen pull it to shore and sit down to divide the fish: the good ones go into their buckets, the worthless ones are thrown away. ⁴⁹ It will be like this at the end of the age: the angels will go out and gather up the evil people from among the good, ⁵⁰ and throw them into the fiery furnace. There they will cry and gnash their teeth."

New and Old Truths

⁵¹ "Do you understand these things?" Jesus asked them. "Yes," they answered. ⁵² So he replied, "This means, then, that every teacher of the Law who becomes a disciple in the Kingdom of heaven is like a homeowner who takes new and old things out of his storage room."

Jesus Rejected at Nazareth
(Also Mark 6.1–6; Luke 4.16–30)

⁵³ When Jesus finished telling these parables, he left that place ⁵⁴ and went back to his home town. He taught in their synagogue, and those who heard him were amazed. "Where did he get such wisdom?" they asked. "And what about his miracles? ⁵⁵ Isn't he the carpenter's son? Isn't Mary his mother, and aren't James, Joseph, Simon, and Judas his brothers? ⁵⁶ Aren't all his sisters living here? Where did he get all this?" ⁵⁷ And so they rejected him. Jesus said to them: "A prophet is respected everywhere except in his home town and by his own fam-. ily." ⁵⁸ He did not perform many miracles there because they did not have faith.

The Death of John the Baptist
(Also Mark 6.14–29; Luke 9.7–9)

14 It was at that time that Herod, the ruler of Galilee, heard about Jesus. ² "He is really John the Baptist who has come back to life," he told his officials. "That is why these powers are at work in him."

³ For Herod had ordered John's arrest, and had him

tied up and put in prison. He did this because of Herodias, his brother Philip's wife. ⁴ John the Baptist kept telling Herod, "It isn't right for you to marry her!" ⁵ Herod wanted to kill him, but he was afraid of the Jewish people, because they considered John to be a prophet.

⁶ On Herod's birthday the daughter of Herodias danced in front of the whole group. Herod was so pleased ⁷ that he promised her: "I swear that I will give you anything you ask for!" ⁸ At her mother's suggestion she asked him, "Give me right here the head of John the Baptist on a plate!" ⁹ The king was sad, but because of the promise he had made in front of all his guests he gave orders that her wish be granted. ¹⁰ So he had John beheaded in prison. ¹¹ The head was brought in on a plate and given to the girl, who took it to her mother. ¹² John's disciples came, got his body, and buried it; then they went and told Jesus.

Jesus Feeds the Five Thousand
(Also Mark 6.30–44; Luke 9.10–17; John 6.1–14)

¹³ When Jesus heard the news, he left that place in a boat and went to a lonely place by himself. The people heard about it, left their towns, and followed him by land. ¹⁴ Jesus got out of the boat, and when he saw the large

crowd his heart was filled with pity for them, and he healed their sick.

15 That evening his disciples came to him and said, "It is already very late, and this is a lonely place. Send the people away and let them go to the villages and buy food for themselves." 16 "They don't have to leave," answered Jesus. "You yourselves give them something to eat." 17 "All we have here are five loaves and two fish," they replied. 18 "Bring them here to me," Jesus said. 19 He ordered the people to sit down on the grass; then he took the five loaves and the two fish, looked up to heaven, and gave thanks to God. He broke the loaves and gave them to the disciples, and the disciples gave them to the people. 20 Everyone ate and had enough. Then the disciples took up twelve baskets full of what was left over. 21 The number of men who ate was about five thousand, not counting the women and children.

Jesus Walks on the Water
(Also Mark 6.45–52; John 6.15–21)

22 Then Jesus made the disciples get into the boat and go ahead of him to the other side of the lake, while he sent the people away. 23 After sending the people away, he went up a hill by himself to pray. When evening came, Jesus was there alone; 24 by this time the boat was far out in the lake, tossed about by the waves, for the wind was blowing against it. 25 Between three and six o'clock in the morning Jesus came to them, walking on the water. 26 When the disciples saw him walking on the water they were terrified. "It's a ghost!" they said, and screamed with fear. 27 Jesus spoke to them at once. "Courage!" he said. "It is I. Don't be afraid!" 28 Then Peter spoke up. "Lord," he said, "if it is really you, order me to come out on the water to you." 29 "Come!" answered Jesus. So Peter got out of the boat and started walking on the water to Jesus. 30 When he noticed the wind, however, he was afraid, and started to sink down in the water. "Save me, Lord!" he cried. 31 At once Jesus reached out and grabbed him and said, "How little faith you have! Why did you doubt?" 32 They both got back into the boat, and the wind died down. 33 The disciples in the boat worshipped Jesus. "Truly you are the Son of God!" they exclaimed.

Jesus Heals the Sick in Gennesaret
(Also Mark 6.53–56)

34 They crossed the lake and came to land at Gennesaret, 35 where the people recognized Jesus. So they sent for the sick people in all the surrounding country and brought them to Jesus. 36 They begged him to let the sick at least touch the edge of his cloak; and all who touched it were made well.

The Teaching of the Ancestors
(Also Mark 7.1–13)

15 Then some Pharisees and teachers of the Law came to Jesus from Jerusalem and asked him: 2 "Why is it that your disciples disobey the teaching handed down by our ancestors? They don't wash their hands in the proper way before they eat!" 3 Jesus answered: "And why do you disobey God's command and follow your own teaching? 4 For God said, 'Honour your father and mother,' and 'Anyone who says bad things about his father or mother must be put to death.' 5 But you teach that if a person has something he could use to help his father or mother, but says, 'This belongs to God,' 6 he does not need to honour his father. This is how you disregard God's word to follow your own teaching. 7 You hypocrites! How right Isaiah was when he prophesied about you!

8 'These people, says God, honour me with
their words,
But their heart is really far away from me.
9 It is no use for them to worship me,
Because they teach man-made commandments as though they were God's rules!' "

The Things that Make a Person Unclean
(Also Mark 7.14–23)

10 Then Jesus called the crowd to him and said to them: "Listen, and understand! 11 It is not what goes into a person's mouth that makes him unclean; rather, what comes out of it makes him unclean."

12 Then the disciples came to him and said, "Do you know that the Pharisees had their feelings hurt by what you said?" 13 "Every plant which my Father in heaven did not plant will be pulled up," answered Jesus. 14 "Don't

worry about them! They are blind leaders; and when one blind man leads another, both fall in the ditch." ¹⁵ Peter spoke up, "Tell us what this parable means." ¹⁶ Jesus said to them: "You are still no more intelligent than the others. ¹⁷ Don't you understand? Anything that goes into a person's mouth goes into his stomach and then out of the body. ¹⁸ But the things that come out of the mouth come from the heart; such things make a man unclean. ¹⁹ For from his heart come the evil ideas which lead him to kill, commit adultery, and do other immoral things; to rob, lie, and slander others. ²⁰ These are the things that make a man unclean. But to eat without washing your hands as they say you should — this does not make a man unclean."

A Woman's Faith
(Also Mark 7.24–30)

²¹ Jesus left that place and went off to the territory near the cities of Tyre and Sidon. ²² A Canaanite woman who lived in that region came to him. "Son of David, sir!" she cried. "Have mercy on me! My daughter has a demon and is in a terrible condition." ²³ But Jesus did not say a word to her. His disciples came to him and begged him, "Send her away! She is following us and making all this noise!" ²⁴ Then Jesus replied, "I have been sent only to the lost sheep of the people of Israel." ²⁵ At this the woman came and fell at his feet. "Help me, sir!" she said.

26 Jesus answered, "It isn't right to take the children's food and throw it to the dogs." 27 "That is true, sir," she answered; "but even the dogs eat the leftovers that fall from their masters' table." 28 So Jesus answered her: "You are a woman of great faith! What you want will be done for you." And at that very moment her daughter was healed.

Jesus Heals Many People

29 Jesus left that place and went along by Lake Galilee. He climbed a hill and sat down. 30 Large crowds came to him, bringing with them the lame, the blind, the crippled,

the dumb, and many other sick people, whom they placed at Jesus' feet; and he healed them. 31 The people were amazed as they saw the dumb speaking, the crippled whole, the lame walking, and the blind seeing; and they praised the God of Israel.

Jesus Feeds the Four Thousand
(Also Mark 8.1–10)

32 Jesus called his disciples to him and said: "I feel sorry for these people, because they have been with me for three days and now have nothing to eat. I don't want to send them away without feeding them, because they might faint on their way home." 33 The disciples asked him, "Where will we find enough food in this desert to feed this crowd?" 34 "How much bread do you have?" Jesus asked. "Seven loaves," they answered, "and a few small fish." 35 So Jesus ordered the crowd to sit down on

the ground. [36] Then he took the seven loaves and the fish, gave thanks to God, broke them and gave them to the disciples, and the disciples gave them to the people. [37] They all ate and had enough. The disciples took up seven baskets full of pieces left over. [38] The number of men who ate was four thousand, not counting the women and children.

[39] Then Jesus sent the people away, got into a boat, and went to the territory of Magadan.

The Demand for a Miracle
(Also Mark 8.11–13; Luke 12.54–56)

16 Some Pharisees and Sadducees came to Jesus. They wanted to trap him, so they asked him to perform a miracle for them, to show God's approval. [2] But Jesus answered: "When the sun is setting you say, 'We are going to have fine weather, because the sky is red.' [3] And early in the morning you say, 'It is going to rain, because the sky is red and dark.' You can predict the weather by looking at the sky; but you cannot interpret the signs concerning these times! [4] How evil and godless are the people of this day!" Jesus added. "You ask me for a miracle? No! The only miracle you will be given is the miracle of Jonah." So he left them and went away.

The Yeast of the Pharisees and Sadducees
(Also Mark 8.14–21)

[5] When the disciples crossed over to the other side of the lake, they forgot to take any bread. [6] Jesus said to them, "Look out, and be on your guard against the yeast of the Pharisees and Sadducees." [7] They started discussing among themselves: "He says this because we didn't bring any bread." [8] Jesus knew what they were saying, so he asked them: "Why are you discussing among yourselves about not having any bread? How little faith you have! [9] Don't you understand yet? Don't you remember when I broke the five loaves for the five thousand men? How many baskets did you fill? [10] And what about the seven loaves for the four thousand men? How many baskets did you fill? [11] How is it that you don't understand that I was not talking to you about bread? Guard yourselves from the yeast of the Pharisees and Sadducees!" [12] Then the disciples understood that he was not telling them to guard

themselves from the yeast used in bread, but from the teaching of the Pharisees and Sadducees.

Peter's Declaration about Jesus
(Also Mark 8.27–30; Luke 9.18–21)

¹³ Jesus went to the territory near the town of Caesarea Philippi, where he asked his disciples, "Who do men say the Son of Man is?" ¹⁴ "Some say John the Baptist," they answered. "Others say Elijah, while others say Jeremiah or some other prophet." ¹⁵ "What about you?" he asked them. "Who do you say I am?" ¹⁶ Simon Peter answered, "You are the Messiah, the Son of the living God." ¹⁷ "Simon, son of John, you are happy indeed!" answered Jesus. "For this truth did not come to you from any human being, but it was given to you directly by my Father in heaven. ¹⁸ And so I tell you: you are a rock, Peter, and on this rock I will build my church. Not even death will ever be able to overcome it. ¹⁹ I will give you the keys of the Kingdom of heaven: what you prohibit on earth will be prohibited in heaven; what you permit on earth will be permitted in heaven." ²⁰ Then Jesus ordered his disciples that they were not to tell anyone that he was the Messiah.

Jesus Speaks about His Suffering and Death
(Also Mark 8.31—9.1; Luke 9.22–27)

²¹ From that time on Jesus began to say plainly to his disciples: "I must go to Jerusalem and suffer much from the elders, the chief priests, and the teachers of the Law. I will be put to death, and on the third day I will be raised to life." ²² Peter took him aside and began to rebuke him. "God forbid it, Lord!" he said. "This must never happen to you!" ²³ Jesus turned around and said to Peter: "Get away from me, Satan! You are an obstacle in my way, for these thoughts of yours are men's thoughts, not God's!"

²⁴ Then Jesus said to his disciples: "If anyone wants to come with me, he must forget himself, carry his cross, and follow me. ²⁵ For the man who wants to save his own life will lose it; but the man who loses his life for my sake will find it. ²⁶ Will a man gain anything if he wins the whole world but loses his life? Of course not! There is nothing a man can give to regain his life. ²⁷ For the Son of Man is about to come in the glory of his Father with his angels,

and then he will repay everyone according to his deeds.
²⁸ Remember this! There are some here who will not die
until they have seen the Son of Man come as King."

The Transfiguration
(Also Mark 9.2–13; Luke 9.28–36)

17 Six days later Jesus took with him Peter, and the
brothers James and John, and led them up a high
mountain by themselves. ² As they looked on, a change
came over him: his face became as bright as the sun, and
his clothes as white as light. ³ Then the three disciples saw
Moses and Elijah talking with Jesus. ⁴ So Peter spoke up
and said to Jesus, "Lord, it is a good thing that we are
here; if you wish, I will make three tents here, one for
you, one for Moses, and one for Elijah." ⁵ While he was
talking, a shining cloud came over them and a voice said
from the cloud: "This is my own dear Son, with whom
I am well pleased — listen to him!" ⁶ When the disciples
heard the voice they were so terrified that they threw

themselves face down to
the ground. ⁷ Jesus came
to them and touched
them. "Get up," he said.
"Don't be afraid!" ⁸ So
they looked up and saw
no one else except Jesus.

⁹ As they came down
the mountain Jesus or-
dered them: "Don't tell
anyone about this vision
you have seen until the
Son of Man has been
raised from death."
¹⁰ Then the disciples
asked Jesus, "Why do
the teachers of the Law
say that Elijah has to
come first?" ¹¹ "Elijah
does indeed come first,"
answered Jesus, "and he
will get everything ready.
¹² But I tell you this:

Elijah has already come and people did not recognize him, but treated him just as they pleased. In the same way the Son of Man will also be mistreated by them." 13 Then the disciples understood that he was talking to them about John the Baptist.

Jesus Heals a Boy with a Demon
(Also Mark 9.14–29; Luke 9.37–43a)

14 When they returned to the crowd, a man came to Jesus, knelt before him, 15 and said: "Sir, have mercy on my son! He is epileptic and has such terrible fits that he often falls in the fire or in the water. 16 I brought him to your disciples, but they could not heal him." 17 Jesus answered: "How unbelieving and wrong you people are! How long must I stay with you? How long do I have to put up with you? Bring the boy here to me!" 18 Jesus commanded the demon and it went out, so that the boy was healed at that very moment.

19 Then the disciples came to Jesus in private and asked him, "Why couldn't we drive the demon out?" 20 "It was because you do not have enough faith," answered Jesus. "Remember this! If you have faith as big as a mustard seed, you can say to this hill, 'Go from here to there!' and it will go. You could do anything! [21 But only prayer and fasting can drive this kind out; nothing else can.]"

Jesus Speaks again about His Death
(Also Mark 9.30–32; Luke 9.43b–45)

22 When the disciples all came together in Galilee, Jesus said to them: "The Son of Man is about to be handed over to men 23 who will kill him; but on the third day he will be raised to life." The disciples became very sad.

Payment of the Temple Tax

24 When Jesus and his disciples came to Capernaum, the collectors of the Temple tax came to Peter and asked, "Does your teacher pay the Temple tax?" 25 "Of course," Peter answered. When Peter went into the house, Jesus spoke up first: "Simon, what is your opinion? Who pays duties or taxes to the kings of this world? The citizens of the country or the foreigners?" 26 "The foreigners," answered Peter. "Well, then," replied Jesus, "that means that the citizens don't have to pay. 27 But we don't want to offend these people. So go to the lake and drop in a line; pull up the first fish you hook, and in its mouth you

will find a coin worth enough for my Temple tax and yours; take it and pay them our taxes."

Who Is the Greatest?
(Also Mark 9.33–37; Luke 9.46–48)

18 At that moment the disciples came to Jesus, asking, "Who is the greatest in the Kingdom of heaven?" [2] Jesus called a child, had him stand in front of them, [3] and said: "Remember this! Unless you change and become like children, you will never enter the Kingdom of heaven. [4] The greatest in the Kingdom of heaven is the one who humbles himself and becomes like this child. [5] And the person who welcomes in my name one such child as this, welcomes me."

Temptations to Sin
(Also Mark 9.42–48; Luke 17.1–2)

[6] "As for these little ones who believe in me — it would be better for a man to have a large millstone tied round his neck and be drowned in the deep sea, than for him to cause one of them to turn away from me. [7] How terrible for the world that there are things that make people turn away! Such things will always happen — but how terrible for the one who causes them!

[8] "If your hand or your foot makes you turn away, cut it off and throw it away! It is better for you to enter life without a hand or foot than to keep both hands and feet and be thrown into the eternal fire. [9] And if your eye makes you turn away, take it out and throw it away! It is better for you to enter life with only one eye than to keep both eyes and be thrown into the fire of hell."

The Parable of the Lost Sheep
(Also Luke 15.3–7)

[10] "See that you don't despise any of these little ones. Their angels in heaven, I tell you, are always in the presence of my Father in heaven. [[11] For the Son of Man came to save the lost.]

[12] "What do you think? What will a man do who has one hundred sheep and one of them gets lost? He will leave the other ninety-nine grazing on the hillside and go to look for the lost sheep. [13] When he finds it, I tell you, he feels far happier over this one sheep than over the

ninety-nine that did not get lost. ¹⁴ In just the same way your Father in heaven does not want any of these little ones to be lost."

A Brother Who Sins

¹⁵ "If your brother sins against you, go to him and show him his fault. But do it privately, just between yourselves. If he listens to you, you have won your brother back. ¹⁶ But if he will not listen to you, take one or two other persons with you, so that 'every accusation may be upheld by the testimony of two or three witnesses,' as the scripture says. ¹⁷ But if he will not listen to them, then tell the whole thing to the church. And then, if he will not listen to the church, treat him as though he were a foreigner or a tax collector."

Prohibiting and Permitting

18 "And so I tell all of you: what you prohibit on earth will be prohibited in heaven; what you permit on earth will be permitted in heaven.

19 "And I tell you more: whenever two of you on earth agree about anything you pray for, it will be done for you by my Father in heaven. 20 For where two or three come together in my name, I am there with them."

The Parable of the Unforgiving Servant

21 Then Peter came to Jesus and asked, "Lord, how many times can my brother sin against me and I have to forgive him? Seven times?" 22 "No, not seven times," answered Jesus, "but seventy times seven. 23 Because the Kingdom of heaven is like a king who decided to check on his servants' accounts. 24 He had just begun to do so when one of them was brought in who owed him millions of pounds. 25 He did not have enough to pay his debt, so his master ordered him to be sold as a slave, with his wife and his children and all that he had, in order to pay the debt. 26 The servant fell on his knees before his master.

'Be patient with me,' he begged, 'and I will pay you everything!' 27 The master felt sorry for him, so he forgave him the debt and let him go.

28 "The man went out and met one of his fellow servants who owed him a few pounds. He grabbed him and started choking him. 'Pay back what you owe me!' he said. 29 His

fellow servant fell down and begged him, 'Be patient with me and I will pay you back!' ³⁰ But he would not; instead, he had him thrown into jail until he should pay the debt. ³¹ When the other servants saw what had happened, they were very upset, and went to their master and told him everything. ³² So the master called the servant in. 'You worthless slave!' he said. 'I forgave you the whole amount you owed me, just because you asked me to. ³³ You should

have had mercy on your fellow servant, just as I had mercy on you.' ³⁴ The master was very angry, and he sent the servant to jail to be punished until he should pay back the whole amount." ³⁵ And Jesus concluded, "That is how my Father in heaven will treat you if you do not forgive your brother, every one of you, from your heart."

Jesus Teaches about Divorce
(Also Mark 10.1–12)

19 When Jesus finished saying these things, he left Galilee and went back to the territory of Judea, on the other side of the Jordan river. ² Large crowds followed him, and he healed them there.

³ Some Pharisees came to him and tried to trap him by asking, "Does our Law allow a man to divorce his wife for any and every reason?" ⁴ Jesus answered: "Haven't you read this scripture? 'In the beginning the Creator made them male and female, ⁵ and said, "For this reason a man will leave his father and mother and unite with his wife, and the two will become one." ' ⁶ So they are no longer two, but one. Man must not separate, then, what God has joined together." ⁷ The Pharisees asked him, "Why, then,

did Moses give the commandment for a man to give his wife a divorce notice and send her away?" 8 Jesus answered: "Moses gave you permission to divorce your wives because you are so hard to teach. But it was not this way at the time of creation. 9 I tell you, then, that any man who divorces his wife, and she has not been unfaithful, commits adultery if he marries some other woman."

10 His disciples said to him, "If this is the way it is between a man and his wife, it is better not to marry." 11 Jesus answered: "This teaching does not apply to everyone, but only to those to whom God has given it. 12 For there are different reasons why men cannot marry: some, because they were born that way; others, because men made them that way; and others do not marry because of the Kingdom of heaven. Let him who can do it accept this teaching."

Jesus Blesses Little Children
(Also Mark 10.13–16; Luke 18.15–17)

13 Some people brought children to Jesus for him to place his hands on them and pray, but the disciples scolded those people. 14 Jesus said, "Let the children come to me, and do not stop them, because the Kingdom of heaven belongs to such as these." 15 He placed his hands on them and left.

The Rich Young Man
(Also Mark 10.17–31; Luke 18.18–30)

16 Once a man came to Jesus. "Teacher," he asked, "what good thing must I do to receive eternal life?" 17 "Why do you ask me concerning what is good?" answered Jesus. "There is only One who is good. Keep the commandments if you want to enter life." 18 "What commandments?" he asked. Jesus answered: "Do not murder; do not commit adultery; do not steal; do not lie; 19 honour your father and mother; and love your neighbour as yourself." 20 "I have obeyed all these commandments," the young man replied. "What else do I need to do?" 21 Jesus said to him, "If you want to be perfect, go and sell all you have and give the money to the poor, and you will have riches in heaven; then come and follow me." 22 When the young man heard this he went away sad, because he was very rich.

23 Jesus then said to his disciples: "It will be very hard, I tell you, for a rich man to enter the Kingdom of heaven. 24 I tell you something else: it is much harder for a rich man to enter the Kingdom of God than for a camel to go through the eye of a needle." 25 When the disciples heard this they were completely amazed. "Who can be saved, then?" they asked. 26 Jesus looked straight at them and answered, "This is impossible for men; but for God everything is possible."

27 Then Peter spoke up. "Look," he said, "we have left everything and followed you. What will we have?" 28 Jesus said to them: "I tell you this: when the Son of Man sits on his glorious throne in the New Age, then you twelve followers of mine will also sit on thrones, to judge the twelve tribes of Israel. 29 And every one who has left houses or brothers or sisters or father or mother or children or fields for my sake, will receive a hundred times more, and will be given eternal life. 30 But many who now are first will be last, and many who now are last will be first."

The Workers in the Vineyard

20 "The Kingdom of heaven is like the owner of a vineyard who went out early in the morning to hire some men to work in his vineyard. 2 He agreed to pay them the regular wage, a silver coin a day, and sent them

to work in his vineyard. ³ He went out again to the market place at nine o'clock and saw some men standing there doing nothing, ⁴ so he told them, 'You also go to work in the vineyard, and I will pay you a fair wage.' ⁵ So they went. Then at twelve o'clock and again at three o'clock he did the same thing. ⁶ It was nearly five o'clock when he went to the market place and saw some other men still standing there. 'Why are you wasting the whole day here doing nothing?' he asked them. ⁷ 'It is because no one hired us,' they answered. 'Well, then, you also go to work in the vineyard,' he told them.

⁸ "When evening came, the owner told his foreman, 'Call the workers and pay them their wages, starting with those who were hired last, and ending with those who were hired first.' ⁹ The men who had begun to work at five o'clock were paid a silver coin each. ¹⁰ So when the men who were the first to be hired came to be paid, they thought they would get more — but they too were given a silver coin each. ¹¹ They took their money and started grumbling against the employer. ¹² 'These men who were hired last worked only one hour,' they said, 'while we put up with a whole day's work in the hot sun — yet you paid them the same as you paid us!' ¹³ 'Listen, friend,' the owner answered one of them. 'I have not cheated you. After all, you agreed to do a day's work for a silver coin. ¹⁴ Now, take your pay and go home. I want to give this man who was hired last as much as I have given you. ¹⁵ Don't I have the right to do as I wish with my own money? Or are you jealous simply because I am generous?' " ¹⁶ And Jesus added, "So those who are last will be first, and those who are first will be last."

Jesus Speaks a Third Time about His Death
(Also Mark 10.32–34; Luke 18.31–34)

¹⁷ As Jesus was going up to Jerusalem he took the twelve disciples aside and spoke to them privately, as they walked along. ¹⁸ "Listen," he told them, "we are going up to Jerusalem, where the Son of Man will be handed over to the chief priests and the teachers of the Law. They will condemn him to death ¹⁹ and then hand him over to the Gentiles, who will make fun of him, whip him, and nail him to the cross; and on the third day he will be raised to life."

A Mother's Request
(Also Mark 10.35–45)

20 Then the mother of Zebedee's sons came to Jesus with her sons, bowed before him, and asked him for a favour. 21 "What do you want?" Jesus asked her. She answered, "Promise that these two sons of mine will sit at your right and your left when you are King." 22 "You don't know what you are asking for," Jesus answered them. "Can you drink the cup that I am about to drink?" "We can," they answered. 23 "You will indeed drink from my cup," Jesus told them, "but I do not have the right to choose who will sit at my right and my left. These places belong to those for whom my Father has prepared them."

24 When the other ten disciples heard about this they became angry with the two brothers. 25 So Jesus called them all together to him and said: "You know that the rulers of the people have power over them, and the leaders rule over them. 26 This, however, is not the way it shall be among you. If one of you wants to be great, he must be the servant of the rest; 27 and if one of you wants to be first, he must be your slave — 28 like the Son of Man, who did not come to be served, but to serve and to give his life to redeem many people."

Jesus Heals Two Blind Men
(Also Mark 10.46–52; Luke 18.35–43)

29 As they were leaving Jericho a large crowd followed Jesus. 30 Two blind men who were sitting by the road heard that Jesus was passing by, so they began to shout, "Son of David! Have mercy on us, sir!" 31 The crowd scolded them and told them to be quiet. But they shouted even more loudly, "Son of David! Have mercy on us, sir!" 32 Jesus stopped and called them. "What do you want me to do for you?" he asked them. 33 "Sir," they answered, "we want you to open our eyes!" 34 Jesus had pity on them and touched their eyes; at once they were able to see, and followed him.

The Triumphant Entry into Jerusalem
(Also Mark 11.1–11; Luke 19.28–40; John 12.12–19)

21 As they approached Jerusalem, they came to Bethphage, at the Mount of Olives. There Jesus sent two of the disciples on ahead 2 with these instructions:

"Go to the village there ahead of you, and at once you will find a donkey tied up and her colt with her. Untie them and bring them to me. ³ And if anyone says anything, tell him, 'The Master needs them'; and he will let them go at once."

⁴ This happened to make come true what the prophet had said:

⁵ "Tell the city of Zion:
Now your king is coming to you,
He is gentle and rides on a donkey,
He rides on a colt, the foal of a donkey."

⁶ So the disciples went ahead and did what Jesus had told them to do: ⁷ they brought the donkey and the colt, threw their cloaks over them, and Jesus got on. ⁸ A great crowd of people spread their cloaks on the road, while others cut branches from the trees and spread them on the road. ⁹ The crowds walking in front of Jesus and the

crowds walking behind began to shout, "Praise to David's Son! God bless him who comes in the name of the Lord! Praise be to God!"

¹⁰ When Jesus entered Jerusalem the whole city was thrown in an uproar. "Who is he?" the people asked.

11 "This is the prophet Jesus, from Nazareth of Galilee," the crowds answered.

Jesus Goes to the Temple
(Also Mark 11.15–19; Luke 19.45–48; John 2.13–22)

12 Jesus went into the Temple and drove out all those who bought and sold in the Temple; he overturned the tables of the money-changers and the stools of those who sold pigeons, 13 and said to them: "It is written in the Scriptures that God said, 'My house will be called a house of prayer.' But you are making it a hideout for thieves!"

14 The blind and the crippled came to him in the Temple and he healed them. 15 The chief priests and the teachers of the Law became angry when they saw the wonderful things he was doing, and the children shouting and crying in the Temple, "Praise to David's Son!" 16 So they said to Jesus, "Do you hear what they are saying?" "Indeed I do," answered Jesus. "Haven't you ever read the scripture that says, 'You have trained children and babies to offer perfect praise'?" 17 Jesus left them and went out of the city to Bethany, where he spent the night.

Jesus Curses the Fig Tree
(Also Mark 11.12–14, 20–24)

18 On his way back to the city, the next morning, Jesus was hungry. 19 He saw a fig tree by the side of the road and went to it, but found nothing on it except leaves. So he said to the tree, "You will never again bear fruit!" At once the fig tree dried up. 20 The disciples saw this and were astounded. "How did the fig tree dry up so quickly?" they asked. 21 "Remember this!" Jesus answered. "If you believe, and do not doubt, you will be able to do what I have done to this fig tree; not only this, you will even be able to say to this hill, 'Get up and throw yourself in the sea,' and it will. 22 If you believe, you will receive whatever you ask for in prayer."

The Question about Jesus' Authority
(Also Mark 11.27–33; Luke 20.1–8)

23 Jesus came back to the Temple; and as he taught, the chief priests and the Jewish elders came to him and asked, "What right do you have to do these things? Who gave you this right?" 24 Jesus answered them: "I will ask you

just one question, and if you give me an answer I will tell you what right I have to do these things. 25 Where did John's right to baptize come from: from God or from man?" They started to argue among themselves: "What shall we say? If we answer, 'From God,' he will say to us, 'Why, then, did you not believe John?' 26 But if we say, 'From man,' we are afraid of what the people might do, because they are all convinced that John was a prophet." 27 So they answered Jesus, "We do not know." And he said to them, "Neither will I tell you, then, by what right I do these things."

The Parable of the Two Sons

28 "Now, what do you think? There was a man who had two sons. He went to the older one and said, 'Son, go work in the vineyard today.' 29 'I don't want to,' he answered, but later he changed his mind and went to the vineyard. 30 Then the father went to the other son and said the same thing. 'Yes, sir,' he answered, but he did not go. 31 Which one of the two did what his father wanted?" "The older one," they answered. "And I tell you this," Jesus said to them. "The tax collectors and the prostitutes are going into the Kingdom of God ahead of you. 32 For John the Baptist came to you showing you the right path to take, and you would not believe him; but the tax collectors and the prostitutes believed him. Even when you saw this you did not change your minds later on and believe him."

The Parable of the Tenants in the Vineyard
(Also Mark 12.1–12; Luke 20.9–19)

33 "Listen to another parable," Jesus said. "There was a landowner who planted a vineyard, put a fence round it, dug a hole for the winepress, and built a tower. Then he rented the vineyard to tenants and left home on a journey. 34 When the time came to harvest the grapes he sent his slaves to the tenants to receive his share. 35 The tenants grabbed his slaves, beat one, killed another, and stoned another. 36 Again the man sent other slaves, more than the first time, and the tenants treated them the same way. 37 Last of all he sent them his son. 'Surely they will respect my son,' he said. 38 But when the tenants saw the son they said to themselves, 'This is the owner's son. Come

on, let us kill him, and we will get his property!' [39] So
they grabbed him, threw him out of the vineyard, and
killed him.

[40] "Now, when the owner of the vineyard comes, what
will he do to those tenants?" Jesus asked. [41] "He will
certainly kill those evil men," they answered, "and rent
the vineyard out to other tenants, who will give him his
share of the harvest at the right time." [42] Jesus said to
them, "Haven't you ever read what the Scriptures say?

'The stone which the builders rejected as
    worthless
Turned out to be the most important stone.
This was done by the Lord,
How wonderful it is!'

[43] And so I tell you," added Jesus, "the Kingdom of God
will be taken away from you and be given to a people
who will produce the proper fruits. [[44] Whoever falls on
this stone will be broken to pieces; and if the stone falls
on someone it will crush him to dust.]"

[45] The chief priests and the Pharisees heard Jesus' parables and knew that he was talking about them, [46] so they
tried to arrest him. But they were afraid of the crowds,
who considered Jesus to be a prophet.

The Parable of the Wedding Feast
(Also Luke 14.15-24)

22 Jesus again used parables in talking to the people.
[2] "The Kingdom of heaven is like a king who prepared a wedding feast for his son. [3] He sent his servants
to tell the invited guests to come to the feast, but they did
not want to come. [4] So he sent other servants with the
message: 'Tell the guests, "My feast is ready now; my
steers and prize calves have been butchered, and everything is ready. Come to the wedding feast!" ' [5] But the
invited guests paid no attention and went about their business: one went off to his farm, the other to his store,
[6] while others grabbed the servants, beat them, and killed
them. [7] The king was very angry, and sent his soldiers
and killed those murderers, and burned down their city.
[8] Then he called his servants. 'My wedding feast is ready,'
he said, 'but the people I invited did not deserve it. [9] Now
go to the main streets and invite to the feast as many
people as you find.' [10] So the servants went out into the

streets and gathered all the people they could find, good and bad alike; and the wedding hall was filled with people.

[11] "The king went in to look at the guests and he saw a man who was not wearing wedding clothes. [12] 'Friend, how did you get in here without wedding clothes?' the king asked him. But the man said nothing. [13] Then the king told the servants, 'Tie him up hand and foot and throw him outside in the dark. There he will cry and gnash his teeth.' " [14] And Jesus concluded, "For many are invited, but few are chosen."

The Question about Paying Taxes
(Also Mark 12.13–17; Luke 20.20–26)

[15] The Pharisees went off and made a plan to trap Jesus with questions. [16] Then they sent some of their disciples and some members of Herod's party to Jesus. "Teacher," they said, "we know that you are an honest man: you teach the truth about God's will for man, without worrying about what people think, because you pay no attention to what a man seems to be. [17] Tell us, then, what do you think? Is it against our Law to pay taxes to the Roman Emperor, or not?" [18] Jesus was aware of their evil plan, however, and so he said: "You impostors! Why are you trying to trap me? [19] Show me the coin to pay the tax!" They brought him the coin, [20] and he asked them, "Whose face and name are these?" [21] "The Emperor's," they answered. So Jesus said to them, "Well, then, pay to the Emperor what belongs to him, and pay to God what belongs to God." [22] When they heard this, they were filled with wonder; and they left him and went away.

The Question about Rising from Death
(Also Mark 12.18–27; Luke 20.27–40)

[23] That same day some Sadducees came to Jesus. (They are the ones who say that people will not rise from death.) [24] "Teacher," they said, "Moses taught: 'If a man who has no children dies, his brother must marry the widow so they can have children for the dead man.' [25] Now, there were seven brothers who used to live here. The oldest got married, and died without having children, so he left his widow to his brother. [26] The same thing happened to the second brother, to the third, and finally to all seven.

²⁷ Last of all, the woman died. ²⁸ Now, on the day when the dead are raised to life, whose wife will she be? All of them had married her!"

²⁹ Jesus answered them: "How wrong you are! It is because you don't know the Scriptures or God's power. ³⁰ For when the dead are raised to life they will be like the angels in heaven, and men and women will not marry. ³¹ Now, about the dead being raised: haven't you ever read what God has told you? For he said, ³² 'I am the God of Abraham, the God of Isaac, and the God of Jacob.' This means that he is the God of the living, not of the dead." ³³ When the crowds heard this they were amazed at his teaching.

The Great Commandment
(Also Mark 12.28-34; Luke 10.25-28)

³⁴ When the Pharisees heard that Jesus had silenced the Sadducees, they came together, ³⁵ and one of them, a teacher of the Law, tried to trap him with a question. ³⁶ "Teacher," he asked, "which is the greatest commandment in the Law?" ³⁷ Jesus answered, " 'You must love the Lord your God with all your heart, and with all your soul, and with all your mind.' ³⁸ This is the greatest and the most important commandment. ³⁹ The second most important commandment is like it: 'You must love your neighbor as yourself.' ⁴⁰ The whole Law of Moses and the teachings of the prophets depend on these two commandments."

The Question about the Messiah
(Also Mark 12.35-37; Luke 20.41-44)

⁴¹ When the Pharisees gathered together, Jesus asked them: ⁴² "What do you think about the Messiah? Whose descendant is he?" "He is David's descendant," they answered. ⁴³ "Why, then," Jesus asked, "did the Spirit inspire David to call him 'Lord'? For David said,

⁴⁴ 'The Lord said to my Lord:
   Sit here at my right side,
   Until I put your enemies under your feet.'
⁴⁵ If, then, David called him 'Lord,' how can the Messiah be David's descendant?" ⁴⁶ No one was able to answer Jesus a single word, and from that day on no one dared ask him any more questions.

Jesus Warns against the Teachers of the Law and the Pharisees
(Also Mark 12.38–39; Luke 11.43, 46; 20.45–46)

23 Then Jesus spoke to the crowds and to his disciples. 2 "The teachers of the Law and the Pharisees," he said, "are the authorized interpreters of Moses' Law. 3 So you must obey and follow everything they tell you to do; do not, however, imitate their actions, because they do not practice what they preach. 4 They fix up heavy loads and tie them on men's backs, yet they aren't willing even to lift a finger to help them carry those loads. 5 They do everything just so people will see them. See how big are the containers with scripture verses on their foreheads and arms, and notice how long are the hems of their cloaks! 6 They love the best places at feasts and the reserved seats in the synagogues; 7 they love to be greeted with respect in the market places and have people call them 'Teacher.' 8 You must not be called 'Teacher,' for you are all brothers of one another and have only one Teacher. 9 And you must not call anyone here on earth 'Father,' for you have only the one Father in heaven. 10 Nor should you be called 'Leader,' because your one and only leader is the Messiah. 11 The greatest one among you must be your servant. 12 And whoever makes himself great will be humbled, and whoever humbles himself will be made great."

Jesus Condemns Their Hypocrisy
(Also Mark 12.40; Luke 11.39–42, 44, 52; 20.47)

13 "How terrible for you, teachers of the Law and Pharisees! Impostors! You lock the door to the Kingdom of heaven in men's faces, but you yourselves will not go in, and neither will you let people in who are trying to go in!

[14 "How terrible for you, teachers of the Law and Pharisees! Impostors! You take advantage of widows and rob them of their homes, and then make a show of saying long prayers! Because of this your punishment will be all the worse!]

15 "How terrible for you, teachers of the Law and Pharisees! Impostors! You sail the seas and cross whole countries to win one convert; and when you succeed, you make him twice as deserving of going to hell as you yourselves are!

¹⁶ "How terrible for you, blind guides! You teach, 'If a man swears by the Temple he isn't bound by his vow; but if he swears by the gold in the Temple, he is bound.' ¹⁷ Blind fools! Which is more important, the gold or the Temple which makes the gold holy? ¹⁸ You also teach, 'If a man swears by the altar he isn't bound by his vow; but if he swears by the gift on the altar, he is bound.' ¹⁹ How blind you are! Which is more important, the gift or the altar which makes the gift holy? ²⁰ So then, when a man swears by the altar he is swearing by it and by all the gifts on it; ²¹ and when a man swears by the Temple he is swearing by it and by God, the one who lives there; ²² and when a man swears by heaven he is swearing by God's throne and by him who sits on it.

²³ "How terrible for you, teachers of the Law and Pharisees! Impostors! You give to God one tenth even of the seasoning herbs, such as mint, dill, and cummin, but you neglect to obey the really important teachings of the Law, such as justice and mercy and honesty. These you should practice, without neglecting the others. ²⁴ Blind guides! You strain a fly out of your drink, but swallow a camel!

²⁵ "How terrible for you, teachers of the Law and Pharisees! Impostors! You clean the outside of your cup and plate, while the inside is full of things you have got by violence and selfishness. ²⁶ Blind Pharisee! Clean what is inside the cup first, and then the outside will be clean too!

²⁷ "How terrible for you, teachers of the Law and Pharisees! Impostors! You are like whitewashed tombs, which look fine on the outside, but are full of dead men's bones and rotten stuff on the inside. ²⁸ In the same way, on the outside you appear to everybody as good, but inside you are full of lies and sins."

Jesus Predicts Their Punishment
(Also Luke 11.47–51)

²⁹ "How terrible for you, teachers of the Law and Pharisees! Impostors! You make fine tombs for the prophets, and decorate the monuments of those who lived good lives, ³⁰ and you say, 'If we had lived long ago in the time of our ancestors, we would not have done what they did and killed the prophets.' ³¹ So you actually admit that you are the descendants of those who murdered the proph-

ets! ³² Go on, then, and finish up what your ancestors started! ³³ Snakes, and sons of snakes! How do you expect to escape from being condemned to hell? ³⁴ And so I tell you: I will send you prophets and wise men and teachers; you will kill some of them, nail others to the cross, and whip others in your synagogues, and chase them from town to town. ³⁵ As a result, the punishment for the murder of all innocent men will fall on you, from the murder of innocent Abel to the murder of Zechariah, Barachiah's son, whom you murdered between the Temple and the altar. ³⁶ I tell you indeed: the punishment for all these will fall upon the people of this day!"

Jesus' Love for Jerusalem
(Also Luke 13.34–35)

³⁷ "O Jerusalem, Jerusalem! You kill the prophets and stone the messengers God has sent you! How many times have I wanted to put my arms round all your people, just as a hen gathers her chicks under her wings, but you would not let me! ³⁸ Now your home will be completely forsaken. ³⁹ From now on you will never see me again, I tell you, until you say, 'God bless him who comes in the name of the Lord.' "

Jesus Speaks of the Destruction of the Temple
(Also Mark 13.1–2; Luke 21.5–6)

24 Jesus left and was going away from the Temple when his disciples came to him to show him the Temple's buildings. ² "Yes," he said, "you may well look at all these. I tell you this: not a single stone here will be left in its place; every one of them will be thrown down."

Troubles and Persecutions
(Also Mark 13.3–13; Luke 21.7–19)

³ As Jesus sat on the Mount of Olives, the disciples came to him in private. "Tell us when all this will be," they asked, "and what will happen to show that it is the time for your coming and the end of the age."

⁴ Jesus answered: "Watch out, and do not let anyone fool you. ⁵ Because many men will come in my name, saying, 'I am the Messiah!' and fool many people. ⁶ You are going to hear the noise of battles close by and the

news of battles far away; but, listen, do not be troubled. Such things must happen, but they do not mean that the end has come. 7 One country will fight another country, one kingdom will attack another kingdom. There will be famines and earthquakes everywhere. 8 All these things are like the first pains of childbirth.

9 "Then men will arrest you and hand you over to be punished, and you will be put to death. All mankind will hate you because of me. 10 Many will give up their faith at that time; they will betray each other and hate each other. 11 Then many false prophets will appear and fool many people. 12 Such will be the spread of evil that many people's love will grow cold. 13 But the person who holds out to the end will be saved. 14 And this Good News about the Kingdom will be preached through all the world, for a witness to all mankind — and then will come the end."

The Awful Horror
(Also Mark 13.14–23; Luke 21.20–24)

15 "You will see 'The Awful Horror,' of which the prophet Daniel spoke, standing in the holy place." (Note to the reader: understand what this means!) 16 "Then those who are in Judea must run away to the hills. 17 The man who is on the roof of his house must not take the time to go down and get his belongings from the house. 18 The man who is in the field must not go back to get his cloak. 19 How terrible it will be in those days for women who are pregnant, and for mothers who have little babies! 20 Pray to God that you will not have to run away during the winter or on a Sabbath! 21 For the trouble at that time will be far more terrible than any there has ever been, from the beginning of the world to this very day. Nor will there ever be anything like it. 22 But God has already reduced the number of days; had he not done so, nobody would survive. For the sake of his chosen people, however, God will reduce the days.

23 "Then, if anyone says to you, 'Look, here is the Messiah!' or 'There he is!' — do not believe him. 24 For false Messiahs and false prophets will appear; they will perform great signs and wonders for the purpose of deceiving God's chosen people, if possible. 25 Listen! I have told you this ahead of time.

26 "Or, if people should tell you, 'Look, he is out in the

desert!' — don't go there; or if they say, 'Look, he is hiding here!' — don't believe it. ²⁷ For the Son of Man will come like the lightning which flashes across the whole sky from the east to the west.

²⁸ "Wherever there is a dead body the vultures will gather."

The Coming of the Son of Man
(Also Mark 13.24–27; Luke 21.25–28)

²⁹ "Soon after the trouble of those days the sun will grow dark, the moon will no longer shine, the stars will fall from heaven, and the powers in space will be driven from their course. ³⁰ Then the sign of the Son of Man will appear in the sky; then all the tribes of earth will weep, and they will see the Son of Man coming on the clouds of heaven with power and great glory. ³¹ The great trumpet will sound, and he will send out his angels to the four corners of the earth, and they will gather his chosen people from one end of the world to the other."

The Lesson of the Fig Tree
(Also Mark 13.28–31; Luke 21.29–33)

³² "Let the fig tree teach you a lesson. When its branches become green and tender, and it starts putting out leaves, you know that summer is near. ³³ In the same way, when you see all these things, you will know that the time is near, ready to begin. ³⁴ Remember this! All these things will happen before the people now living have all died. ³⁵ Heaven and earth will pass away; my words will never pass away."

No One Knows the Day and Hour
(Also Mark 13.32–37; Luke 17.26–30, 34–36)

³⁶ "No one knows, however, when that day and hour will come — neither the angels in heaven, nor the Son; the Father alone knows. ³⁷ The coming of the Son of Man will be like what happened in the time of Noah. ³⁸ Just as in the days before the Flood, people ate and drank, men and women married, up to the very day Noah went into the ark; ³⁹ yet they did not know what was happening until the Flood came and swept them all away. That is how it will be when the Son of Man comes. ⁴⁰ At that time two men will be working in the field: one will be taken away, the other will be left behind. ⁴¹ Two

women will be at the mill grinding meal: one will be taken away, the other will be left behind. ⁴² Watch out, then, because you do not know what day your Lord will come. ⁴³ Remember this: if the man of the house knew the time when the thief would come, he would stay awake and not let the thief break into his house. ⁴⁴ For this reason, then, you also must be always ready, because the Son of Man will come at an hour when you are not expecting him."

The Faithful or the Unfaithful Servant
(Also Luke 12.41–48)

⁴⁵ "Who, then, is the faithful and wise servant? He is the one whom his master has placed in charge of the other servants, to give them their food at the proper time. ⁴⁶ How happy is that servant if his master finds him doing this when he comes home! ⁴⁷ Indeed, I tell you, the master will put that servant in charge of all his property. ⁴⁸ But if he is a bad servant, he will tell himself, 'My master will not come back for a long time,' ⁴⁹ and he will begin to beat his fellow servants, and eat and drink with drunkards. ⁵⁰ Then that servant's master will come back some day when he does not expect him and at a time he does not know; ⁵¹ the master will cut him to pieces, and make him share the fate of the impostors. There he will cry and gnash his teeth."

The Parable of the Ten Girls

25 "On that day the Kingdom of heaven will be like ten girls who took their oil lamps and went out to

meet the bridegroom. [2] Five of them were foolish, and the other five were wise. [3] The foolish ones took their lamps but did not take any extra oil with them, [4] while the wise ones took containers full of oil with their lamps. [5] The bridegroom was late in coming, so the girls began to nod and fall asleep.

[6] "It was already midnight when the cry rang out, 'Here is the bridegroom! Come and meet him!' [7] The ten girls woke up and trimmed their lamps. [8] Then the foolish ones said to the wise ones, 'Let us have some of your oil, because our lamps are going out.' [9] 'No, indeed,' the wise ones answered back, 'there is not enough for you and us. Go to the store and buy some for yourselves.' [10] So the foolish girls went off to buy some oil, and while they were gone the bridegroom arrived. The five girls who were ready went in with him to the wedding feast, and the door was closed.

[11] "Later the other girls arrived. 'Sir, sir! Let us in!' they cried. [12] 'But I really don't know you,' the bridegroom answered." [13] And Jesus concluded, "Watch out, then, because you do not know the day or hour."

The Parable of the Three Servants
(Also Luke 19.11–27)

[14] "It will be like a man who was about to leave home on a journey: he called his servants and put them in charge of his property. [15] He gave to each one according to his ability: to one he gave five thousand pounds, to the other two thousand pounds, and to the other one thousand pounds. Then he left on his trip. [16] The servant who had received five thousand pounds went at once and invested his money and earned another five thousand pounds. [17] In the same way the servant who received two thousand pounds earned another two thousand pounds. [18] But the servant who received one thousand pounds went off, dug a hole in the ground, and hid his master's money.

[19] "After a long time the master of those servants came back and settled accounts with them. [20] The servant who had received five thousand pounds came in and handed over the other five thousand pounds. 'You gave me five thousand pounds, sir,' he said. 'Look! Here are another five thousand pounds that I have earned.' [21] 'Well done, good and faithful servant!' said his master. 'You have been

faithful in managing small amounts, so I will put you in charge of large amounts. Come on in, and share my happiness!' ²² Then the servant who had been given two thousand pounds came in and said, 'You gave me two thousand pounds, sir. Look! Here are another two thousand pounds that I have earned.' ²³ 'Well done, good and faithful servant!' said his master. 'You have been faithful in managing small amounts, so I will put you in charge of large amounts. Come on in and share my happiness!' ²⁴ Then the servant who had received one thousand pounds came in and said: 'Sir, I know you are a hard man: you reap harvests where you did not plant, and gather crops where you did not scatter seed. ²⁵ I was afraid, so I went off and hid your money in the ground. Look! Here is what belongs to you.' ²⁶ 'You bad and lazy servant!' his master said. 'You knew, did you, that I reap harvests where I did not plant, and gather crops where I did not scatter seed? ²⁷ Well, then, you should have deposited my money in the bank, and I would have received it all back with interest when I returned. ²⁸ Now, take the money away from him and give it to the one who has ten thousand pounds. ²⁹ For to every one who has, even more will be given, and he will have more than enough; but the one who has nothing, even the little he has will be taken away from him. ³⁰ As for this useless servant — throw him outside in the darkness; there he will cry and gnash his teeth.' "

The Final Judgment

³¹ "When the Son of Man comes as King, and all the angels with him, he will sit on his royal throne, ³² and all the earth's people will be gathered before him. Then he will divide them into two groups, just as a shepherd separates the sheep from the goats: ³³ he will put the sheep at his right and the goats at his left. ³⁴ Then the King will say to the people on his right: 'You who are blessed by my Father: come! Come and receive the kingdom which has been prepared for you ever since the creation of the world. ³⁵ I was hungry and you fed me, thirsty and you gave me drink; I was a stranger and you received me in your homes, ³⁶ naked and you clothed me; I was sick and you took care of me, in prison and you visited me.' ³⁷ The righteous will then answer him: 'When, Lord, did we

ever see you hungry and feed you, or thirsty and give you drink? [38] When did we ever see you a stranger and welcome you in our homes, or naked and clothe you? [39] When did we ever see you sick or in prison, and visit you?' [40] The King will answer back, 'I tell you, indeed, whenever you did this for one of the least important of these brothers of mine, you did it for me!'

[41] "Then he will say to those on his left: 'Away from me, you who are under God's curse! Away to the eternal fire which has been prepared for the Devil and his angels! [42] I was hungry but you would not feed me, thirsty but you would not give me drink; [43] I was a stranger but you would not welcome me in your homes, naked but you would not clothe me; I was sick and in prison but you would not take care of me.' [44] Then they will answer him: 'When, Lord, did we ever see you hungry, or thirsty, or a stranger, or naked, or sick, or in prison, and we would not help you?' [45] The King will answer them back, 'I tell you, indeed, whenever you refused to help one of these least important ones, you refused to help me.' [46] These, then, will be sent off to eternal punishment; the righteous will go to eternal life."

The Plot against Jesus
(Also Mark 14.1–2; Luke 22.1–2; John 11.45–53)

26 When Jesus had finished teaching all these things, he said to his disciples, [2] "In two days, as you know, it will be the Feast of Passover, and the Son of Man will be handed over to be nailed to the cross."

[3] Then the chief priests and the Jewish elders met together in the palace of Caiaphas, the High Priest, [4] and made plans to arrest Jesus secretly and put him to death. [5] "We must not do it during the feast," they said, "or the people will riot."

Jesus Anointed at Bethany
(Also Mark 14.3–9; John 12.1–8)

[6] While Jesus was at the house of Simon the leper, in Bethany, [7] a woman came to him with an alabaster jar filled with an expensive perfume, which she poured on Jesus' head as he was eating. [8] The disciples saw this and became angry. "Why all this waste?" they asked. [9] "This perfume could have been sold for a large amount and the money given to the poor!" [10] Jesus was aware of what they

were saying and said to them: "Why are you bothering this woman? It is a fine and beautiful thing that she has done for me. ¹¹ You will always have poor people with you, but I will not be with you always. ¹² What she did was to pour this perfume on my body to get me ready for burial. ¹³ Now, remember this! Wherever this gospel is preached, all over the world, what she has done will be told in memory of her."

Judas Agrees to Betray Jesus
(Also Mark 14.10–11; Luke 22.3–6)

¹⁴ Then one of the twelve disciples — the one named Judas Iscariot — went to the chief priests ¹⁵ and said, "What will you give me if I hand Jesus over to you?" So they counted out thirty silver coins and gave them to him. ¹⁶ From then on Judas was looking for a good chance to betray Jesus.

Jesus Eats the Passover Meal with His Disciples
(Also Mark 14.12–21; Luke 22.7–14, 21–23; John 13.21–30)

¹⁷ On the first day of the Feast of Unleavened Bread the disciples came to Jesus and asked him, "Where do you want us to get the Passover supper ready for you?" ¹⁸ "Go to a certain man in the city," he said to them, "and tell him: 'The Teacher says, My hour has come; my disciples and I will celebrate the Passover at your house.'" ¹⁹ The disciples did as Jesus had told them and prepared the Passover supper.

²⁰ When it was evening Jesus and the twelve disciples sat down to eat. ²¹ During the meal Jesus said, "I tell you, one of you will betray me." ²² The disciples were very upset and began to ask him, one after the other, "Surely you don't mean me, Lord?" ²³ Jesus answered: "One who dips his bread in the dish with me will betray me. ²⁴ The Son of Man will die as the Scriptures say he will, but how terrible for that man who will betray the Son of Man! It would have been better for that man if he had never been born!" ²⁵ Judas, the traitor, spoke up. "Surely you don't mean me, Teacher?" he asked. Jesus answered, "So you say."

The Lord's Supper
(Also Mark 14.22–26; Luke 22.15–20; 1 Cor. 11.23–25)

²⁶ While they were eating, Jesus took the bread, gave

a prayer of thanks, broke it, and gave to his disciples. "Take and eat it," he said; "this is my body." ²⁷ Then he took the cup, gave thanks to God, and gave it to them. "Drink it, all of you," he said; ²⁸ "for this is my blood, which seals God's covenant, my blood poured out for many for the forgiveness of sins. ²⁹ I tell you, I will never again drink this wine until the day I drink the new wine with you in my Father's Kingdom." ³⁰ Then they sang a hymn and went out to the Mount of Olives.

Jesus Predicts Peter's Denial
(Also Mark 14.27–31; Luke 22.31–34; John 13.36–38)

³¹ Then Jesus said to them: "This very night all of you will run away and leave me, for the scripture says, 'God will kill the shepherd and the sheep of the flock will be scattered.' ³² But after I am raised to life I will go to Galilee ahead of you." ³³ Peter spoke up and said to Jesus, "I will never leave you, even though all the rest do!" ³⁴ "Remember this!" Jesus said to Peter. "Before the cock crows tonight you will say three times that you do not know me." ³⁵ Peter answered, "I will never say I do not know you, even if I have to die with you!" And all the disciples said the same thing.

Jesus Prays in Gethsemane
(Also Mark 14.32–42; Luke 22.39–46)

³⁶ Then Jesus went with his disciples to a place called Gethsemane, and he said to them, "Sit here while I go over there and pray." ³⁷ He took with him Peter, and Zebedee's two sons. Grief and anguish came over him, ³⁸ and he said to them, "The sorrow in my heart is so great

that it almost crushes me. Stay here and watch with me."
39 He went a little farther on, threw himself face down to
the ground, and prayed, "My Father, if it is possible, take
this cup away from me! But not what I want, but what
you want."

40 Then he returned to the three disciples and found
them asleep; and he said to Peter: "How is it that you
three were not able to watch with me for one hour?
41 Keep watch, and pray, so you will not fall into tempta-
tion. The spirit is willing, but the flesh is weak."

42 Again a second time Jesus went away and prayed,
"My Father, if this cup cannot be taken away unless I
drink it, your will be done." 43 He returned once more
and found the disciples asleep; they could not keep their
eyes open.

44 Again Jesus left them, went away, and prayed the
third time, saying the same words. 45 Then he returned to
the disciples and said: "Are you still sleeping and resting?
Look! The hour has come for the Son of Man to be
handed over to the power of sinful men. 46 Rise, let us
go. Look, here is the man who is betraying me!"

The Arrest of Jesus
(Also Mark 14.43–50; Luke 22.47–53; John 18.3–12)

47 He was still talking when Judas, one of the twelve
disciples, arrived. With him was a large crowd carrying
swords and clubs, sent by the chief priests and the Jewish
elders. 48 The traitor had given the crowd a signal: "The
man I kiss is the one you want. Arrest him!" 49 When
Judas arrived he went straight to Jesus and said, "Peace
be with you, Teacher," and kissed him. 50 Jesus answered,
"Be quick about it, friend!" Then they came up, arrested
Jesus, and held him tight. 51 One of those who were with
Jesus drew his sword and struck at the High Priest's slave,
cutting off his ear. 52 Then Jesus said to him: "Put your
sword back in its place, for all who take the sword will
die by the sword. 53 Don't you know that I could call on
my Father for help and at once he would send me more
than twelve armies of angels? 54 But in that case, how
could the Scriptures come true that say it must happen
in this way?"

55 Then Jesus spoke to the crowd: "Did you have to
come with swords and clubs to capture me, as though

I were an outlaw? Every day I sat down and taught in the Temple, and you did not arrest me. [56] But all this has happened to make come true what the prophets wrote in the Scriptures."

Then all the disciples left him and ran away.

Jesus before the Council
(Also Mark 14.53–65; Luke 22.54–55, 63–71; John 18.13–14, 19–24)

[57] Those who had arrested Jesus took him to the house of Caiaphas, the High Priest, where the teachers of the Law and the elders had gathered together. [58] Peter followed him from a distance, as far as the courtyard of the High Priest's house. He went into the courtyard and sat down with the guards, to see how it would all come out. [59] The chief priests and the whole Council tried to find some false evidence against Jesus, to put him to death; [60] but they could not find any, even though many came up and told lies about him. Finally two men stepped forward [61] and said, "This man said, 'I am able to tear down God's Temple and three days later build it back up.' "

[62] The High Priest stood up and said to Jesus, "Have you no answer to give to this accusation against you?" [63] But Jesus kept quiet. Again the High Priest spoke to him: "In the name of the living God, I now put you on oath: tell us if you are the Messiah, the Son of God." [64] Jesus answered him: "So you say. But I tell all of you: from this time on you will see the Son of Man sitting at the right side of the Almighty, and coming on the clouds of heaven!" [65] At this the High Priest tore his clothes and said: "Blasphemy! We don't need any more witnesses! Right here you have heard his wicked words! [66] What do you think?" They answered, "He is guilty, and must die."

[67] Then they spat in his face and beat him; and those who slapped him [68] said, "Prophesy for us, Messiah! Tell us who hit you!"

Peter Denies Jesus
(Also Mark 14.66–72; Luke 22.56–62; John 18.15–18, 25–27)

[69] Peter was sitting outside in the courtyard, when one of the High Priest's servant girls came to him and said, "You, too, were with Jesus of Galilee." [70] But he denied it in front of them all. "I don't know what you are talking about," he answered, [71] and went on out to the en-

trance of the courtyard. Another servant girl saw him and said to the men there, "He was with Jesus of Nazareth." 72 Again Peter denied it, and answered, "I swear that I don't know that man!" 73 After a little while the men standing there came to Peter. "Of course you are one of them," they said. "After all, the way you speak gives you away!" 74 Then Peter made a vow: "May God punish me if I am not telling the truth! I do not know that man!" Just then a cock crowed, 75 and Peter remembered what Jesus had told him, "Before the cock crows, you will say three times that you do not know me." He went out and wept bitterly.

Jesus Taken to Pilate
(Also Mark 15.1; Luke 23.1–2; John 18.28–32)

27 Early in the morning all the chief priests and the Jewish elders made their plan against Jesus to put him to death. 2 They put him in chains, took him, and handed him over to Pilate, the Governor.

The Death of Judas
(Also Acts 1.18–19)

3 When Judas, the traitor, saw that Jesus had been condemned, he repented and took back the thirty silver coins to the chief priests and the elders. 4 "I have sinned by betraying an innocent man to death!" he said. "What do we care about that?" they answered. "That is your business!" 5 Judas threw the money into the sanctuary and left them; then he went off and hanged himself.

6 The chief priests picked up the money and said, "This is blood money, and it is against our Law to put it in the Temple treasury." 7 After reaching an agreement about it, they used the money to buy Potter's Field, as a cemetery for foreigners. 8 That is why that field is called "Field of Blood" to this very day.

9 Then what the prophet Jeremiah had said came true: "They took the thirty silver coins (the amount the people of Israel had agreed to pay for him), 10 and used them to buy the potter's field, as the Lord commanded me."

Pilate Questions Jesus
(Also Mark 15.2–5; Luke 23.3–5; John 18.33–38)

11 Jesus stood before the Governor, who questioned him. "Are you the king of the Jews?" he asked. "So you say,"

answered Jesus. [12] He said nothing, however, to the accusations of the chief priests and elders. [13] So Pilate said to him, "Don't you hear all these things they accuse you of?" [14] But Jesus refused to answer a single word, so that the Governor was greatly surprised.

Jesus Sentenced to Death
(Also Mark 15.6–15; Luke 23.13–25; John 18.39—19.16)

[15] At every Passover Feast the Governor was in the habit of setting free any prisoner the crowd asked for. [16] At that time there was a well-known prisoner named Jesus Barabbas. [17] So when the crowd gathered, Pilate asked them, "Which one do you want me to set free for you, Jesus Barabbas or Jesus called the Christ?" [18] He knew very well that they had handed Jesus over to him because they were jealous.

[19] While Pilate was sitting in the judgment hall, his wife sent him a message: "Have nothing to do with that innocent man, because in a dream last night I suffered much on account of him."

[20] The chief priests and the elders persuaded the crowds to ask Pilate to set Barabbas free and have Jesus put to death. [21] But the Governor asked them, "Which one of these two do you want me to set free for you?" "Barabbas!" they answered. [22] "What, then, shall I do with Jesus called the Christ?" Pilate asked them. "Nail him to the cross!" they all answered. [23] But Pilate asked, "What crime has he committed?" Then they started shouting at the top of their voices, "Nail him to the cross!" [24] When Pilate saw it was no use to go on, but that a riot might break out, he took some water, washed his hands in front of the crowd, and said, "I am not responsible for the death of this man! This is your doing!" [25] The whole crowd answered back, "Let the punishment for his death fall on us and on our children!" [26] Then Pilate set Barabbas free for them; he had Jesus whipped and handed him over to be nailed to the cross.

The Soldiers Make Fun of Jesus
(Also Mark 15.16–20; John 19.2–3)

[27] Then Pilate's soldiers took Jesus into the Governor's palace, and the whole company gathered around him. [28] They stripped off his clothes and put a scarlet robe on

him. 29 Then they made a crown out of thorny branches
and put it on his head, and put a stick in his right hand;
then they knelt before him and made fun of him. "Long
live the King of the Jews!" they said. 30 They spat on him,
and took the stick and hit him over the head. 31 When
they finished making fun of him, they took the robe off
and put his own clothes back on him, and then led him
out to nail him to the cross.

Jesus Nailed to the Cross
(Also Mark 15.21–32; Luke 23.26–43; John 19.17–27)

32 As they were going out they met a man from Cyrene
named Simon, and they forced him to carry Jesus' cross.
33 They came to a place called Golgotha, which means
"The Place of the Skull." 34 There they offered him wine
to drink, mixed with gall; after tasting it, however, he
would not drink it.

35 They nailed him to the cross, and then divided his
clothes among them by throwing dice. 36 After that they
sat there and watched him. 37 Above his head they put
the written notice of the accusation against him: "This is
Jesus, the King of the Jews." 38 Then they nailed two
bandits to crosses with Jesus, one on his right and the
other on his left.

39 People passing by shook their heads and threw insults
at Jesus: 40 "You were going to tear down the Temple and
build it up in three days! Save yourself, if you are God's
Son! Come on down from the cross!" 41 In the same way
the chief priests and the teachers of the Law and the
elders made fun of him: 42 "He saved others but he cannot save himself! Isn't he the King of Israel? If he will
come down off the cross now, we will believe in him!
43 He trusts in God and says he is God's Son. Well, then,
let us see if God wants to save him now!" 44 Even the
bandits who had been crucified with him insulted him
in the same way.

The Death of Jesus
(Also Mark 15.33–41; Luke 23.44–49; John 19.28–30)

45 At noon the whole country was covered with darkness, which lasted for three hours. 46 At about three
o'clock Jesus cried out with a loud shout, *Eli, Eli, lema
sabachthani?* which means, "My God, my God, why did

you abandon me?" [47] Some of the people standing there heard him and said, "He is calling for Elijah!" [48] One of them ran up at once, took a sponge, soaked it in wine, put it on the end of a stick, and tried to make him drink it. [49] But the others said, "Wait, let us see if Elijah is coming to save him!" [50] Jesus again gave a loud cry, and breathed his last.

[51] Then the curtain hanging in the Temple was torn in two, from top to bottom. The earth shook, the rocks split apart, [52] the graves broke open, and many of God's people who had died were raised to life. [53] They left the graves; and after Jesus rose from death they went into the Holy City, where many people saw them.

[54] When the army officer and the soldiers with him who were watching Jesus saw the earthquake and everything else that happened, they were terrified and said, "He really was the Son of God!" [55] There were many women there, looking on from a distance, who had followed Jesus from Galilee and helped him. [56] Among them were Mary Magdalene, Mary the mother of James and Joseph, and the mother of Zebedee's sons.

The Burial of Jesus
(Also Mark 15.42–47; Luke 23.50–56; John 19.38–42)

[57] When it was evening, a rich man from Arimathea arrived; his name was Joseph, and he also was a disciple

of Jesus. [58] He went into the presence of Pilate and asked for the body of Jesus. Pilate gave orders for the body to be given to Joseph. [59] So Joseph took it, wrapped it in a new linen sheet, [60] and placed it in his own grave, which he had just recently dug out of the rock. Then he rolled

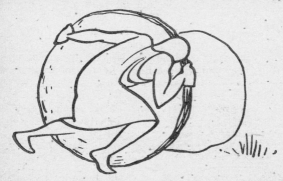

a large stone across the entrance to the grave and went away. [61] Mary Magdalene and the other Mary were sitting there, facing the grave.

The Guard at the Grave

[62] On the next day — that is, the day following Friday — the chief priests and the Pharisees met with Pilate [63] and said: "Sir, we remember that while that liar was still alive he said, 'I will be raised to life after three days.' [64] Give orders, then, for the grave to be safely guarded until the third day, so that his disciples will not be able to go and steal him, and then tell the people, 'He was raised from death.' This last lie would be even worse than the first one." [65] "Take a guard," Pilate told them; "go and guard the grave as best you can." [66] So they left, and made the grave secure by putting a seal on the stone and leaving the guard on watch.

The Resurrection
(Also Mark 16.1–10; Luke 24.1–12; John 20.1–10)

28 After the Sabbath, as Sunday morning was dawning, Mary Magdalene and the other Mary went to look at the grave. [2] Suddenly there was a strong earthquake; an angel of the Lord came down from heaven,

rolled the stone away, and sat on it. ³ His appearance was like lightning and his clothes were white as snow. ⁴ The guards were so afraid that they trembled and became like dead men.

⁵ The angel spoke to the women. "You must not be afraid," he said. "I know you are looking for Jesus, who was nailed to the cross. ⁶ He is not here; he has risen, just as he said. Come here and see the place where he lay. ⁷ Quickly, now, go and tell his disciples: 'He has been raised from death, and now he is going to Galilee ahead of you; there you will see him!' Remember what I have

told you." ⁸ So they left the grave in a hurry, afraid and yet filled with joy, and ran to tell his disciples.

⁹ Suddenly Jesus met them and said, "Peace be with you." They came up to him, took hold of his feet, and worshipped him. ¹⁰ "Do not be afraid," Jesus said to them. "Go and tell my brothers to go to Galilee, and there they will see me."

The Report of the Guard

¹¹ While the women went on their way, some of the soldiers guarding the grave went back to the city and told the chief priests everything that had happened. ¹² The chief priests met with the elders and made their plan; they gave a large sum of money to the soldiers ¹³ and said: "You are to say that his disciples came during the night and stole his body while you were asleep. ¹⁴ And if the

Governor should hear of this, we will convince him and you will have nothing to worry about." [15] The guards took the money and did what they were told to do. To this very day that is the report spread round by the Jews.

Jesus Appears to His Disciples
(Also Mark 16.14–18; Luke 24.36–49; John 20.19–23; Acts 1.6–8)

[16] The eleven disciples went to the hill in Galilee where Jesus had told them to go. [17] When they saw him they worshipped him, even though some of them doubted. [18] Jesus drew near and said to them: "I have been given all authority in heaven and on earth. [19] Go, then, to all peoples everywhere and make them my disciples: baptize them in the name of the Father and of the Son and of the Holy Spirit, [20] and teach them to obey everything I have commanded you. And remember! I will be with you always, to the end of the age."

GOOD NEWS FOR MODERN MAN

The New Testament in Today's English Version

This translation in contemporary language, published originally in the United States by the American Bible Society, has met with wide approval. Nearly thirty million copies have been sold throughout the world.

Editions available in the United Kingdom published by Collins and Fontana Books.

New Testament T.E.V. illustrated 608 pages

Cloth cover	60p
Rexine cover	£1·38

Published jointly by the British and Foreign Bible Society and the National Bible Society of Scotland in association with Fontana Books.

New Testament illustrated paperback		25p
„ „ paperback without illustrations		15p
Single Books with illustrations		
Matthew	80 pages	3p
Mark	64 pages	3p
Luke	84 pages	3p
John	64 pages	3p
Philippians	16 pages	2p
Each Gospel available in large type		12p